FLORIDA
TEST PREP

FSA

GRADE 4

ELA
ENGLISH
LANGUAGE
ARTS

Origins Publications

We help students develop their higher-order thinking skills while also improving their chances of admission into gifted and accelerated-learner programs.

Our goal is to unleash and nurture the genius in every student. We do this by offering educational and test prep materials that are fun, challenging and provide a sense of accomplishment.

Please contact us with any questions.

info@originspublications.com

Copyright © 2018 by Origins Publications

Written and Edited by: FSA Test Prep Team

ISBN 13: 978-1-948255-04-2

The Florida Standards Assessment (FSA®) is a registered trademark of the Florida Department of Education, which is not affiliated with Origins Publications. The Florida Department of Education has not endorsed the contents of this book.

Origins Publications
New York, NY, USA
Email:info@originspublications.com

TABLE OF CONTENTS

INTRODUCTION

The Florida Standards Assessments

The Florida Standard Assessments (FSA) are important tests designed to assess whether students are meeting the rigorous standards that have been implemented in schools across Florida. These standards, or learning goals, outline what students in each grade should learn each year. These standards emphasize just how important the new goals are: they can help show whether students are on the right track to college and beyond, even when the students are years from those life stages.

FSA English Language Arts (ELA) Reading Assessment

Fourth grade students in Florida are required to take the FSA ELA reading assessments, which are aligned with the Language Arts Florida Standards (LAFS). The tests are designed to determine whether students have mastered grade-level appropriate reading skills.

The ELA reading assessment for Grades 4-10 is administered in April-May. The test is computer based, although pencil-paper format is available for students with specific disabilities.

The ELA reading assessment for Grades 3-5 consists of two 80-minute sessions. Students complete one session per day. The assessment contains 55–66 questions.

Questions are based on reading passages, which may be literary or informational. Students will also respond to some items associated with listening passages. For fourth grade students, passages are between 100-900 words. They may include multimedia elements such as slideshows, charts, graphs, images, etc. Passages often appear in pairs.

Question Format on FSA ELA Assessments

Students taking the ELA reading assessment will be asked to respond to several types of questions. Most question types will likely be familiar to the student, such as multiple-choice questions, where students select the correct response from four answer choices. The ELA reading assessments also contain questions called Technology Enhanced Items (TEIs), including:

Open Response: A student must answer a question in one or two complete sentences within the space, usually an answer box.

Multi-select: A student must select a specified number of answers that s/he thinks best responds to the question.

Editing Task: Students type (or choose from a drop-down menu) a correction for the highlighted word or phrase in a provided text box.

Graphic Response Item Display (GRID): A student must select words or phrases and place them into a graphic organizer or other format.

Evidence-based Selected Response (EBSR): A student must use the reading passage to answer Part A (multiple choice question) and Part B (multiple choice or other format). Part A often asks the student to make an inference, while Part B requires the student to choose the best supporting statement for the inference.

HOW TO USE THIS BOOK

The objective of this book is to provide students, educators, and parents with practice materials focused on the core skills needed to help students succeed on the FSA ELA reading assessment.

A student will fare better on an assessment when s/he has practiced and mastered the skills measured by the test. A student also excels when s/he is familiar with the format and structure of the test. This book helps students do both. Students can review key material by standard through doing the skill-building exercises, as well as take practice tests to become accustomed to how the content is presented and to enhance test-taking skills. By test day, students will feel confident and be adequately prepared to do his or her best.

This Book Includes:

- 228 skill-building exercises organised by standard in order to help students learn and review concepts in the order that they will likely be presented in the classroom. These worksheets also help identify weaknesses, and highlight and strengthen the skills needed to excel on the actual exam. A variety of question types are included in the worksheets to help students build skills in answering questions in multiple formats, so they don't get tripped up by perplexing or unfamiliar question types on test day.

- Our ELA practice tests are based on the official FSA ELA reading assessments released by the test administrator. Our practice tests include similar question types and the same rigorous content found on the official assessments. By using these materials, students will become familiar with the types of items (including Technology Enhanced Items (TEIs) presented in a paper based format) and response formats they may see on the test. One practice test is included at the end of the book. **Another practice test can be downloaded as a PDF online. You will find instructions on accessing this test on page 168.**

- Answer keys with detailed explanations to help students not make the same mistakes again. These explanations help clear up common misconceptions and indicate how students might arrive at an answer to a question.

- The answer explanations for the practice tests also identify the standard/s that the question is assessing. If a student is having difficulty in one area, encourage the student to improve in that area by practicing the specific set of skills in the workbook.

- Test prep tips to help students approach the test strategically and with confidence.

TEST PREP TIPS

First of all, remind your student to pay attention in class throughout the year, asking questions as needed on homework and classwork. The Language Arts curriculum should follow the exact standards and skills that will be tested on the end-of-year assessment.

One of the best ways to prepare for a reading test is by—of course—reading. In the months leading up to the test, students should read a certain amount of pages or minutes weekly from a book that they enjoy. Reading consistently will improve a student's reading comprehension and enhance her vocabulary, two skills that are crucial to success on the exam.

Another extremely effective strategy is to practice, practice, practice. Have your student work on practice questions and complete several full length practice tests. Our practice tests are a great place to start.

However, simply answering the questions and then moving on will not yield much improvement. If a student misses a question, discuss why the correct answer is indeed correct. Come up with alternate approaches to this question type that may work better in the future. Have your student explain his answer to each question. This gives you the opportunity to reinforce logical thinking and correct misconceptions as needed. Plus, it's good practice for finding evidence to support a claim, perhaps the key skill on ELA reading assessments.

Prior to the test, students should have a solid night of sleep and eat a nourishing breakfast.

Avoiding excessive test anxiety is important, so be sure to avoid over-emphasizing the test or inadvertently causing your student to feel too much stress or pressure.

In addition, teach your student general test-taking strategies such as the following:

Narrow down your answer choices by using process of elimination. This involves crossing out obviously wrong answers to increase your chances of finding the correct answer.

If you get stuck on a question, skip it and come back to it after answering easier questions.

Remember that no one is expected to answer every single correction correctly. Don't panic when you get stuck on a question. Take a deep breath and remember that you are intelligent and prepared.

If you follow the tips here, your student should be well on her way to a stress-free and successful performance on this important assessment.

READING: LITERATURE

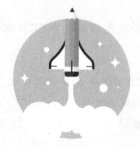

UNDERSTAND TEXT

RL.4.1: Refer to details and examples in a text when explaining what the text says explicitly and when drawing inferences from the text.

Directions: Read the passage and answer the questions below.

Passage 1: Adapted selection from *The Dragon Tamers* (Part 1)
by Edith Nesbit

1 There was once an old, old castle—it was so old that its walls, towers, and arches had crumbled to ruins, and of all its old splendor there were only two little rooms left. It was here that John the farrier had set up his forge. John used the forge to heat and shape metal horseshoes for horses. No one asked any rent for the rooms in the ruin, because, in fact, the castle was abandoned.

2 One day, through the hammering a noise came louder and louder, and the more John and his wife tried not to hear it, the more they had to. It was like the noise of some great creature purring, purring, purring. It came from the great dungeon down below with the broken steps that went down into the dark and ended no one knew where.

3 Eventually, John went to the winding stairs and held up the lantern. Half of it was empty, but the other side was not. It was quite full, and what it was full of was Dragon.

4 The dragon caught John by the leg. As it moved it rattled like a great bunch of keys. As it moved, the castle also heaved with the dragon's mighty movement.

5 "Oh, I'm glad you finally found me, as I should like you to do a job for me," said the dragon. "One of my wings has got some of the screws out of it just above the joint. You mend my wing, and then I'll go out and eat up all the townsfolk, and if you do a really smart job of it, I'll eat you last."

1. What is the greatest danger to John and his family in this story?
    A. The castle is abandoned.
    B. There is no light in the stairwell.
    C. A dragon is living in the castle with John and his family.
    D. John is not paying rent for the two rooms in the castle.

2. Which statement best explains why John does not need to pay money (rent) to live in the castle?
    A. John likes living with the dragon.
    B. The two rooms that the family lives in are cramped.
    C. John offers an important service to the community by making shoes for the town's horses.
    D. No-one collects money for the castle's rent.

3. Re-read this sentence from the text: "There was once an old, old castle—it was so old that its walls, towers, and arches had crumbled to ruins, and of all its old splendor there were only two little rooms left."

What do you think the word splendor means in the above passage?

    A. antiques

    B. magnificence

    C. sweetness

    D. architecture

4. The following question has two parts. First, answer Part A. Then, answer Part B.

Part A

What is the most convincing reason that the dragon wants to be found?

    A. The dragon wants someone to help it fix its wing.

    B. The dragon is concerned that the castle is falling down.

    C. The dragon wants to play tag with John.

    D. The dragon wants John to be scared and leave the castle.

Part B

What evidence from the text best supports your answer in A?

    A. "The dragon caught John by the leg." (Paragraph 4).

    B. "As it moved it rattled like a great bunch of keys." (Paragraph 4).

    C. "...it was so old that its walls, towers, and arches had crumbled to ruins..." (Paragraph 1).

    D. "I should like you to do a job for me," said the dragon. "One of my wings has got some of the screws out of it just above the joint." (Paragraph 5).

Directions: Read the poem and answer the questions below.

St. Patrick's Day
by Jean Blewett

There's an Isle, a green Isle, set in the sea,
  Here's to the Saint that blessed it!
And here's to the billows wild and free
  That for centuries have caressed it!

Here's to the day when the men that roam
  Send longing eyes o'er the water!
Here's to the land that still spells home
  To each loyal son and daughter!

Here's to old Ireland—fair, I ween,
  With the blue skies stretched above her!
Here's to her shamrock warm and green,
  And here's to the hearts that love her!

5. Based on the poem, you can infer that the country is…
    A. attached to other countries
    B. an island
    C. landlocked
    D. very cold

6. How does the poet feel about the country?
    A. The poet feels glad to be away from the country.
    B. The poet once had a lot of fun in the country.
    C. The poet loves and cherishes the country.
    D. The poet wishes there was more to do in the country.

7. What does the word "fair' mostly likely mean in the first line of the final stanza?
    A. beautiful
    B. okay
    C. equal
    D. odd

8. What country is the poem about?
    A. England
    B. Ireland
    C. Russia
    D. Greenland

READING: LITERATURE

DETERMINE THEME & SUMMARIZE TEXT

RL.4.2 Determine a theme of a story, drama, or poem from details in the text; summarize the text.

Directions: Read the poem and answer the questions that follow.

Passage 1: Two Little Kittens
by: Anonymous

Two little kittens, one stormy night,
Began to quarrel, and then to fight;
One had a mouse, the other had none,
And that's the way the quarrel begun.

"I'll have that mouse," said the biggest cat;
"You'll have that mouse? We'll see about that!"
"I will have that mouse," said the tortoise-shell;
And, spitting and scratching, on her sister she fell.

I told you before 'twas a stormy night
When these two little kittens began to fight;
The old woman seized her sweeping broom,
And swept the two kittens right out of the room.

The ground was covered with frost and snow,
And the two little kittens had nowhere to go;
So, they laid them down on the mat at the door,
While the old woman finished sweeping the floor.

Then they crept in, as quiet as mice,
All wet with the snow, and cold as ice,
For they found it was better, that stormy night,
To lie down and sleep than to quarrel and fight.

1. Why are the kittens fighting?
    A. One cat likes storms and the other doesn't.
    B. One cat has a mouse and the other doesn't.
    C. One cat has a bigger mouse than the other.
    D. One cat wants to eat and one wants to play.

READING: LITERATURE

2. There are two parts for this question. First, answer Part A, then Part B.

Part A.

What is the main moral of this poem?

A. It's better to get along than to fight.

B. Don't go outside on a stormy day.

C. It's better to play inside than outside.

D. Kittens should always be quieter than mice.

Part B.

Which piece of evidence from the poem supports your answer from question 2?

A. "The old woman seized her sweeping broom,

And swept the two kittens right out of the room."

B. "I told you before 'twas a stormy night

When these two little kittens began to fight;"

C. "Then they crept in, as quiet as mice,

All wet with the snow, and cold as ice…"

D. "For they found it was better, that stormy night,

To lie down and sleep than to quarrel and fight."

3. In lines 11 and 12, why did the old woman sweep "the two kittens right out of the room?"

_____

_____

_____

_____

4. Summarize this poem. Include details about how the setting contributes to the overall theme of the poem. Support your conclusions with evidence from the text.

_____

_____

_____

_____

_____

Directions: Read the passage and answer the questions below.

Passage 2: I survived

1   In 1971, I was seventeen years old and flying to the Peruvian rainforest to visit my father, a scientist studying plants, animals and their habitats. About thirty minutes into the flight, lightning began striking around the plane, and passengers started screaming.

2   Next, lightning hit the plane, and the airplane ripped in half. I was somehow ejected from the plane, still buckled into my seat. I woke up the next morning with some cuts and a broken collarbone. I was so surprised that I was still alive! Then, I realized how alone I was in the jungle.

3   I didn't have any food with me, but I found a bag of candy that someone must have brought on the plane. I remembered that my father had told me to follow water if I was ever lost in the jungle. I found a stream and started walking beside it.

4   Soon, I ran out of candy. My father also taught me that a lot of the food in the jungle was poisonous, so I just drank lots of water from the stream. By the tenth day, I could barely walk. I knew that I desperately needed food. Eventually, I saw a small hut. I went into the hut and fell asleep.

5   In the morning, the sounds of men's voices woke me. I explained to the men what had happened to me. They gave me food, and I was reunited with my father a day later. Of the 92 passengers on my flight, only I survived.

5. Why is it important to mention that the author is going to visit her father, a scientist studying plants, animals and their habitats?
    A. The author wants to let the reader know that her father's knowledge of the jungle helps save her.
    B. The author wants the reader to know that her father shouldn't have let her fly alone.
    C. It gives the reader interesting background information about the author.
    D. The author wants us to understand that she had a close relationship with her father.

6. Which of the following is one of the main themes of this passage?
    A. Humans can live for weeks without food.
    B. Survival skills can help you stay alive in the wild.
    C. Airplane crashes can be very frightening.
    D. Don't fly in a plane over a jungle.

7. Why does the author include Paragraph 4?

   A. To show that the author might not have survived if she didn't find the hut when she did.

   B. To show how eating too much candy affected the author.

   C. To explain why the author decided to give up.

   D. To show readers that the author shouldn't have gone into a stranger's hut.

8. Only the author survived the plane crash. Summarize how the author survived and stayed alive in the jungle. Include two details from the text.

_____

_____

_____

_____

_____

_____

DESCRIBE CHARACTER, SETTING, AND EVENTS

RL.4.3 Describe in depth a character, setting, or event in a story or drama, drawing on specific details in the text (e.g., a character's thoughts, words, or actions).

Directions: Read the passage and answer the questions below.

Passage 1: The Princess and the Pea
by Hans Christian Andersen

1   ONCE upon a time there was a prince who wanted to marry a princess; but she would have to be a real princess. He travelled all over the world to find one, but nowhere could he get what he wanted. There were princesses enough, but it was difficult to find out whether they were real ones. There was always something about them that was not as it should be. So he came home again and was sad, for he would have liked very much to have a real princess.

2   One evening a terrible storm came on; there was thunder and lightning, and the rain poured down in torrents. Suddenly a knocking was heard at the city gate, and the old king went to open it.

3   There was a princess standing out there in front of the gate. But, good gracious! what a sight the rain and the wind had made her look. The water ran down from her hair and clothes; it ran down into the toes of her shoes and out again at the heels. And yet she said that she was a real princess.

4   Well, we'll soon find that out, thought the old queen. But she said nothing, went into the bed-room, took all the bedding off the bedstead, and laid a pea on the bottom; then she took twenty mattresses and laid them on the pea, and then twenty eider-down beds on top of the mattresses.

5   On this the princess had to lie all night. In the morning she was asked how she had slept.

6   Oh, very badly! said she. I have scarcely closed my eyes all night. Heaven only knows what was in the bed, but I was lying on something hard, so that I am black and blue all over my body. Its horrible!

7   Now they knew that she was a real princess because she had felt the pea right through the twenty mattresses and the twenty eider-down beds.

8   Nobody but a real princess could be as sensitive as that.

9   So the prince asked her to be his wife. Now, he knew that he had married a real princess; and the pea was put in the museum, where it may still be seen, if no one has stolen it.

10   There, that is a true story.

1. Why does the queen require the princess to sleep on twenty mattresses on top of a pea?
   - **A.** She believes that the prince is being too picky about finding a wife.
   - **B.** She wants to prove to the prince that there's no such thing as a true princess.
   - **C.** She wants to determine if the young woman is truly a princess.
   - **D.** She wants to prove that the princess can detect a tiny pea.

2. Which detail from the story best supports the claim that the princess was a real princess?
   - **A.** "But, good gracious! what a sight the rain and the wind had made her look."
   - **B.** "...she had felt the pea right through the twenty mattresses and the twenty eider-down beds."
   - **C.** "...and the pea was put in the museum, where it may still be seen, if no one has stolen it."
   - **D.** "And yet she said that she was a real princess."

3. Based on the events in the story, which word best describes the prince at the end of the story?
   - **A.** satisfied
   - **B.** sleepy
   - **C.** concerned
   - **D.** sad

4. How does the setting and character description in paragraphs 2 and 3 build suspense about the young woman's character? Give evidence from the text to support your answer.

_____

_____

_____

_____

_____

Directions: Read the passage and answer the questions below.

Passage 2: The Ants & the Grasshopper
by Aesop

1 One bright day in late autumn a family of Ants were bustling about in the warm sunshine, drying out the grain they had stored up during the summer, when a starving Grasshopper, his fiddle under his arm, came up and humbly begged for a bite to eat.

2 "What!" cried the Ants in surprise, "haven't you stored anything away for the winter? What in the world were you doing all last summer?"

3 "I didn't have time to store up any food," whined the Grasshopper; "I was so busy making music that before I knew it the summer was gone."

4 The Ants shrugged their shoulders in disgust.

5 "Making music, were you?" they cried. "Very well; now dance!" And they turned their backs on the Grasshopper and went on with their work.

6 There's a time for work and a time for play.

5. Setting is the place or surroundings where a story takes place. Write a phrase that describes the setting in the column titled Phrase that Describes the Setting. Then select two pieces of supporting evidence from the text and write them in the column titled Evidence From "The Ants & the Grasshopper."

Phrase that Describes the Setting	Evidence From "The Ants & the Grasshopper"

6. Reread paragraph 1. The author uses the adjective humbly to describe how the grasshopper approaches the ants. Based on this adjective, how is the grasshopper feeling at this moment?

    A. angry and demanding

    B. meek and embarrassed

    C. happy and full

    D. sympathetic and giving

Directions: Read the short passage and answer the question below.

Dogs used to dig holes and bury their bones to keep them safe from dogs and other animals. Even though most dogs have enough food to eat today, they still want to bury their favorite bones and toys because of their natural instincts.

9. Based on the passage above, make an inference about why dogs today still hide their bones and toys.
   A. They like to save it as a snack for later.
   B. They want to hide them from other dogs.
   C. They think it is a fun game to play with their owners.
   D. They enjoy digging holes and finding bones.

Directions: Read the short passage and answer the question below.

Jerome was about halfway through his math homework when he glanced at his watch. "Oh no!", he said aloud. He threw on his soccer jersey and quickly put on his favorite cleats. He grabbed his soccer bag and sprinted out the door. "Nice of you to join us, Jerome," his soccer coach bellowed as Jerome made his way onto the field.

10. What can you infer based on the evidence in the paragraph?
   A. Jerome is late to soccer practice.
   B. Jerome really loves soccer.
   C. Jerome slept late and missed soccer.
   D. Jerome isn't very organized.

Directions: Read the short passage and answer the question below.

Jasmine saw her friend Allison walking slowly into the classroom. Allison was late again, and she looked upset. She has to walk her younger siblings to daycare each morning on her way to school. The daycare is ¼ of a mile away from her school, and she is usually late to class. Allison needs to wake up early in the morning to walk her siblings to daycare and doesn't get enough sleep at night, which puts her in a bad mood and she is often forgetful. Yesterday she forgot her homework and today she forgot a pencil. Jasmine doesn't want her friend, Allison, to have a bad day at school, so she opens up her pencil case to provide an extra pencil for Allison.

11. Make an inference about why Jasmine is looking for an extra pencil. Explain your answer using evidence from the text.

_____

_____

_____

7. The following question has two parts. First answer Part A. Then, answer Part B.

Part A

What can you infer about the ants in the story?

> **A.** They appreciate the grasshopper's music.
> **B.** They are hopeful that the grasshopper will help them.
> **C.** They believe the grasshopper was foolish.
> **D.** They feel sorry for the grasshopper.

Part B

Which detail from the text supports the answer for Part A?

> **A.** "...a starving Grasshopper, his fiddle under his arm, came up and humbly begged for a bite to eat."
> **B.** "The Ants shrugged their shoulders in disgust."
> **C.** "One bright day in late autumn..."
> **D.** "...a family of Ants were bustling about in the warm sunshine..."

8. When the ants say, "Very well; now dance!" what does it reveal about their belief about the grasshopper's actions over the summer? Use information from the text in your explanation.

_____

_____

_____

_____

_____

DETERMINE WORD MEANING IN TEXT

RL.4.4 Determine the meaning of words and phrases as they are used in a text, including those that allude to significant characters found in mythology (e.g., Herculean).

Directions: Read the passage and answer the questions below.

Passage: A Golden Moment

1   The moment was here. Jessie shook out her arms and leaned left and right, stretching. She took a deep breath, exhaling slowly to blow out the butterflies that had been fluttering in her stomach. She was trying to beat the world record for number of baskets made in one minute while riding a unicycle. She had been practicing for ages. All she needed was one more than the current record of 33.

2   The officials from the World Record Book were ready, stiffly holding their recording sheets, video recorders in hand. Jessie stared at their logs, wondering if her name would ever be in that book. She worried briefly if her Achilles heel would be her downfall—the last time she practiced a cramp in her shoulder kept her from making baskets from the left side. But before she had too much time to worry, the officials called her name. There was no turning back.

3   A particularly stern man with a stopwatch told Jessie to take her place. He towered over Jessie, unsmiling, and examined his clipboard. He frowned as he inspected the stopwatch. Jessie mounted her unicycle, ball in hand. As the man counted down, "In 5, 4, 3, 2, 1, begin!" Jessie cycled around the court, preparing for her first shot. At the official's signal she began shooting.

4   The first 30 shots came easily, but then Jessie missed. And missed again. "This is a catastrophe," she thought miserably. With just 15 seconds to know, Jessie needed to make four more shots. And then, as she'd done a hundred times before, Jessie relaxed her body. 31, 32, 33… the next few shots sailed in. Just one more to go! Shot 34 bounced around the rim, teetering on the edge before falling through the hoop.

5   "Yes!" Jessie and the crowd roared together! She hopped off her bike just in time for her best friend Sam to squeeze her neck. The officials, now smiling, walked over with a ribbon printed with "World Record Holder." The stern official from earlier shook Jessie's hand, "You certainly seem to have the Midas Touch, young lady," he congratulated her.

6   Jessie felt her heart explode with pride. She had done it!

1. What does the word mounted mean in paragraph 3?
    A. attached
    B. rode
    C. climbed on
    D. put away

2. What word or phrase could be substituted for the word catastrophe in paragraph 4?
    A. disaster
    B. lucky break
    C. exciting event
    D. dream

3. In paragraph 4, what effect does the word teetering have on the action of the story?
    A. It makes the reader doubt that Jessie has been practicing.
    B. It adds suspense, as the reader wonders if Jessie will make it.
    C. It advances the plot by telling the reader that Jessie has done this hundreds of times before.
    D. It implies that Jessie will be disappointed in the end.

4. Reread the following sentence.
    "And then, as she'd done a hundred times before, Jessie relaxed her body. 31, 32, 33... the next few shots sailed in."
    What effect does the word sailed have on the meaning of the text?

    _____

    _____

    _____

    _____

5. Reread this sentence from paragraph 1.
    "She took a deep breath, exhaling slowly to blow out the butterflies that had been fluttering in her stomach."
    In the sentence, the phrase "butterflies...fluttering in her stomach" implies that:
    A. Jessie is hungry.
    B. Jessie is nervous.
    C. Jessie needs to stretch more.
    D. Jessie's time is running out.

6. Define the meaning of the word "stern" as it is used in the passage (paragraph 3). Then distinguish two details from the text that best support your understanding of the word and explain how the evidence supports your definition.

Definition:		
	Evidence from the text	**Explanation of how text evidence supports the definition**
#1		
#2		

7. The following question has two parts. First, answer Part A. Then, answer Part B.

Part A

Based on what you know about Jessie from this passage, how might you describe an Achilles heel as the author uses it in paragraph 2?

   A. a weakness

   B. an injured foot

   C. an advantage

   D. a strong arm

Part B

Which detail from the text helps the reader understand the meaning of the phrase Achilles heel in Part A?

   A. "She worried"

   B. "her downfall"

   C. "she practiced"

   D. "her shoulder"

8. What does it mean to have the Midas Touch? How does this reference help the reader understand the task the character faced?

_____

_____

_____

EXPLAIN STRUCTURAL DIFFERENCES BETWEEN POEMS, DRAMA AND PROSE

RL.4.5 Explain major differences between poems, drama, and prose, and refer to the structural elements of poems (e.g., verse, rhythm, meter) and drama (e.g., casts of characters, settings, descriptions, dialogue, stage directions) when writing or speaking about a text.

Directions: Read the passages and answer the questions below.

Passage 1: Adapted excerpt from "Rikki-tikki-tavi" from The Jungle Books, Volume Two.
by Rudyard Kipling

1   This is the story of the great war that Rikki-tikki-tavi fought single-handed, through the bath-rooms of the big bungalow in Segowlee dwelling. Darzee, the tailor-bird, helped him, and Chuchundra, the musk-rat, who never comes out into the middle of the floor, but always creeps round by the wall, gave him advice; but Rikki-tikki did the real fighting.

2   He was a mongoose, rather like a little cat in his fur and his tail, but quite like a weasel in his head and his habits. His eyes and the end of his restless nose were pink; he could scratch himself anywhere he pleased, with any leg, front or back, that he chose to use; he could fluff up his tail till it looked like a bottle-brush, and his war-cry, as he scuttled through the long grass, was: "Rikk-tikk-tikki-tikki-tchk!"

3   One day, a high summer flood washed him out of the burrow where he lived with his father and mother, and carried him, kicking and clucking, down a roadside ditch. He found a little wisp of grass floating there, and clung to it till he lost his senses. When he woke up, he was lying in the hot sun on the middle of a garden path, wet and dirty, and a small boy was saying: "Here's a dead mongoose. Let's have a funeral."

4   "No," said his mother; "let's take him in and dry him. Perhaps he isn't really dead."

5   They took him into the house, and a big man picked him up between his finger and thumb, and said he was not dead but half choked; so they wrapped him in cotton-wool, and warmed him, and he opened his eyes and sneezed.

6   "Now," said the big man (he was an Englishman who had just moved into the bungalow); "don't frighten him, and we'll see what he'll do."

7   It is the hardest thing in the world to frighten a mongoose, because he is so curious. The motto of all the mongoose family is "Run and find out"; and Rikki-tikki was a true mongoose. He looked at the cotton-wool, decided that it was not good to eat, ran all around the table, sat up and put his fur in order, scratched himself, and jumped on the small boy's shoulder.

Passage 2: Dust of Snow
by Robert Frost

> The way a crow
> Shook down on me
> The dust of snow
> From a hemlock tree
>
> Has given my heart
> A change of mood
> And saved some part
> Of a day I had rued.

Passage 3: Excerpt from The Pirates' Adventure

Characters: Pirate Pete, Patchy Parrot, Pegleg Perry, Other Pirates

Act 1

(The crew is on a pirate ship, and just finishing various maintenance tasks.)

Pirate Pete: Ahoy, mateys! It's time to once again return to the deep blue sea!

Pegleg Perry: Yes! We need to find the prince's treasure.

Patchy Parrot: Awk. Treasure?

Pegleg Perry: The prince's treasure is a legend, but only the bravest pirate crew is courageous enough to search for it.

Pirate Pete: The ship is ready, we leave at dawn!

Patchy Parrot: Awk. We leave at dawn!

All: Yo-ho-ho!

1. Read Passage 1 from "Rikki Tikki Tavi." The structure of this text is
    A. poetry
    B. drama
    C. prose.
    D. verse.

2. Passage 2 includes all of the following structural elements EXCEPT?
    A. rhyme
    B. rhythm
    C. stanzas
    D. dialogue

3. How is Passage 1 organized?

    A. paragraphs

    B. stage directions

    C. verses

    D. writing

4. What are the structural elements used in a drama and what purpose do they serve?

    _____

    _____

    _____

    _____

5. What is the function of the dialogue in Passage 1?

    A. It helps the reader understand what is happening.

    B. It gives the writing a consistent rhythm and pattern.

    C. It helps the reader understand the mongoose's point of view.

    D. It tells the reader background knowledge helpful for understanding the story.

6. Re-read passage 3. What is the function of the stage directions in this passage?

    A. They help the reader predict the solution.

    B. They help the reader understand the setting.

    C. They help the reader know characters descriptions.

    D. They help the reader know who is speaking.

7. The following question has two parts. First answer Part A. Then, answer Part B.

Part A

Read the following poem that introduces the story "Rikki-tikki-tavi"(Passage 1). What structural element do the poem and the actual story have in common?

At the hole where he went in
Red-Eye called to Wrinkle-Skin.
Hear what little Red-Eye saith:
"Nag, come up and dance with death!"

Eye to eye and head to head,
(Keep the measure, Nag.)
This shall end when one is dead;
(At thy pleasure, Nag.)

Turn for turn and twist for twist-
(Run and hide thee, Nag.)
Hah! The hooded Death has missed!
(Woe betide thee, Nag!)

    A. rhythm
    B. dialogue
    C. rhyme
    D. stage directions

Part B

Who does much of the poem address?
    A. Rikki-tikki-tavi
    B. Nag
    C. Red-Eye
    D. Wrinkle-Skin

8. Read Passages 1 and 2. Complete the comparison chart by analyzing the text structure to identify and explain the literary format of each passage.

"Rikki Tikki Tavi"	Structural Elements	Text Evidence	Explanation
Literary Format: _____	1. _____ 2. _____	1. _____ 2. _____	1. _____ 2. _____
"Dust of Snow"	**Structural Elements**	**Text Evidence**	**Explanation**
Literary Format: _____	1. _____ 2. _____	1. _____ 2. _____	1. _____ 2. _____

COMPARE AND CONTRAST POINT OF VIEW

RL.4.6 Compare/contrast the point of view from which different stories are narrated, including the difference between first- and third-person narrations.

Directions: Read the passages and answer the questions below.

Passage 1 : Excerpt from The Wonderful Wizard of Oz
by Lyman Frank Baum

1   The Scarecrow found a tree full of nuts and filled Dorothy's basket with them, so that she would not be hungry for a long time. She thought this was very kind and thoughtful of the Scarecrow, but she laughed heartily at the awkward way in which the poor creature picked up the nuts. His padded hands were so clumsy that he dropped almost as many as he put in the basket. But the Scarecrow did not mind how long it took him to fill the basket, for it enabled him to keep away from the fire, as he feared a spark might get into his straw and burn him up.

Passage 2: Adapted Excerpt of the "The Myth of Icarus and Daedelus"

1   There was once a young man named Icarus. He and his father Daedelus were imprisoned by an evil man on an island. They were surrounded by high walls, and the island was surrounded by water.

2   Daedelus was an inventor. He invented wings made from bird feathers and wax. He wanted to use the wings to escape. But because of the wax, the wings would melt if they got hot. So Daedelus warned Icarus not to fly too close to the sun. You can probably guess what happened next.

3   Daedulus and Icarus used the wings to fly away from the island. "Remember," said the father, "never fly very low or very high. The Earth's fog will weigh you down, but the blaze of the sun will melt your feathers apart if you go too near."

4   They escaped across the sea. But Icarus was too excited about flying. He didn't remember his father's instructions and enjoyed the feeling of flying. He flew too close to the hot sun. The wax melted, and he fell into the sea.

5   Daedelus only saw the feathers floating on the water, and knew that Icarus had drowned. He was filled with sadness. He named the nearest island Icaria, in memory of his beloved son. And he never flew again.

1.   From what point of view is the story told in Passage 1?
   A. first-person
   B. second-person
   C. third-person
   D. limited view

READING: LITERATURE

27

2. From what point of view is most of Passage 2 told?

    A. first-person

    B. second-person

    C. third-person

    D. limited view

3. The following question has two parts. First, answer Part A. Then, answer Part B.

Part A

In which paragraph of Passage 2 does the point of view shift to second-person for a moment?

    A. paragraph 2

    B. paragraph 3

    C. paragraph 4

    D. paragraph 5

Part B

What evidence from the text shows you the 2nd person point of view?

    A. "He named the nearest island Icaria, in memory of his beloved son. "

    B. "They escaped across the sea."

    C. "Remember," said the father, "never fly very low or very high."

    D. "You can probably guess what happened next."

4. How would you best describe the narrator in both Passage 1 and Passage 2?

    A. a friend

    B. the Scarecrow

    C. an outside observer

    D. the mythical god

5. What conclusion can be drawn about the author's point of view in Passage 2? How does it relate to the theme? Support your answer with details from the text.

_____

_____

_____

_____

_____

_____

6. An author often uses a point of view called omniscient when the narrator tells the reader what characters are thinking or feeling. Fill in the chart with examples of how the author uses an omniscient point of view in Passage 1 and Passage 2.

"The Wonderful Wizard of Oz"	"The Myth of Icarus and Daedelus"

7. How does the narrator develop Icarus' character in Passage 2?

   A. The narrator shows that Icarus is stubborn and refuses to listen to his father.

   B. The narrator develops Icarus as an evil character.

   C. The narrator presents Icarus as a sympathetic character who we should feel sorry for.

   D. The narrator reveals Icarus' youth and carelessness, which leads to his death.

8. How would Passage 1 change if the story was told from another point of view? Describe the effect on the reader if the point of view changed.

_____

_____

_____

_____

9. Read Passage 2. Now, rewrite the story from a first person point of view.

_____

_____

_____

_____

_____

_____

_____

USE IMAGES TO UNDERSTAND TEXT

RL.4.7 Make connections between the text of a story or drama and a visual or oral presentation of the text, identifying where each version reflects specific descriptions and directions in the text.

Directions: Read the passage and answer the questions below.

Passage 1: Mouse Deer and Tiger

Mouse Deer sang his song as he walked through the forest. He was looking for tasty fruits and roots and shoots. Although he was small, he wasn't afraid of the other bigger animals who wanted to eat him

Then he heard something. Rowr!

There was Tiger!

"Hello, Mouse Deer. I was just getting hungry. Now you can be my lunch."

Mouse Deer didn't want to be lunch. He looked around and thought fast. He saw a mud puddle.

"I'm sorry, Tiger. I can't be your lunch. The King has ordered me to guard his pudding."

"His pudding?" said Tiger.

"Yes. There it is." Mouse Deer pointed to the mud puddle. "It has the best taste in the world. The King doesn't want anyone else to eat it."

Tiger looked longingly at the puddle. "I would like to taste the King's pudding."

"Oh, no, Tiger! The King would be very angry."

"Just one little taste, Mouse Deer! The King will never know."

"Well, all right, Tiger. But first let me run far away, so no one will blame me."

"All right, Mouse Deer, you can go now."

Mouse Deer ran quickly out of sight.

"Imagine!" said Tiger. "The King's pudding!" He took a big mouthful.

Phooey! He spit it out.

"Yuck! Ugh! Bleck! That's no pudding. That's mud!"

Tiger ran through the forest. He caught up with Mouse Deer.

"Mouse Deer, you tricked me once. But now you will be my lunch!"

Mouse Deer looked around and thought fast. He saw a wasp nest in a tree.

"I'm sorry, Tiger. I can't be your lunch. The King has ordered me to guard his drum."

"His drum?" said Tiger.

"Yes. There it is." Mouse Deer pointed to the wasp nest. "It has the best sound in the world. The King doesn't want anyone else to hit it."

Tiger said, "I would like to hit the King's drum."

"Oh, no, Tiger! The King would be very angry."

"Just one little hit, Mouse Deer! The King will never know."

"Well, all right, Tiger. But first let me run far away, so no one will blame me."

"All right, Mouse Deer, you can go now."

Mouse Deer ran quickly out of sight.

"Imagine!" said Tiger. "The King's drum!" He reached up and hit it. The wasps all flew out. They started to sting Tiger.

"Ouch! That's no drum. That's a wasp nest!"

Tiger ran away. But the wasps only followed him!

Tiger came to a stream. He jumped in and stayed underwater as long as he could. At last the wasps went away.

Then Tiger jumped out. He ran through the forest till he found Mouse Deer.

"Mouse Deer, you tricked me once. You tricked me twice. But now you will be my lunch!"

Mouse Deer looked around and thought fast. He saw a cobra! The giant snake was coiled asleep on the ground.

"I'm sorry, Tiger. I can't be your lunch. The King has ordered me to guard his belt."

"His belt?" said Tiger.

"Yes. There it is." Mouse Deer pointed to the cobra. "It's the best belt in the world. The King doesn't want anyone else to wear it."

Tiger said, "I would like to wear the King's belt."

"Oh, no Tiger! The King would be very angry."

"Just for one moment, Mouse Deer! The King will never know."

"Well, all right, Tiger. But first let me run far away, so no one will blame me."

"All right, Mouse Deer, you can go now."

Mouse Deer ran quickly out of sight.

"Imagine!" said Tiger. "The King's belt!" He started to wrap it around himself.

The cobra woke up. It didn't wait for Tiger to finish wrapping. It wrapped itself around Tiger. Then it squeezed him and bit him.

"Ooh! Ow! Yow! That's no belt. That's a cobra! Help! Mouse Deer! Help!"

But Mouse Deer was far away. And as he went, he sang his song.

1. The following question has two parts. First answer Part A. Then, answer Part B.

Part A

Read the passage "Mouse Deer and Tiger." Then view the book cover of a different version of this story. Which statement best explains the connection between the passage and illustration?

    A. The passage describes how the Mouse Deer outsmarts the Tiger, and the illustration reinforces this.
    B. The passage describes the Tiger's intent to eat the Mouse Deer, and the illustration reinforces this idea.
    C. The passage describes how the animals become best friends, and the illustration supports this idea.
    D. The passage describes a rivalry between the Mouse Deer and the Tiger, but the illustration does not support this.

Part B

Which piece of evidence from the passage **best** supports the comparison statement in Part A?
    A. "Hello, Mouse Deer. I was just getting hungry. Now you can be my lunch."
    B. "Tiger ran through the forest. He caught up with Mouse Deer."
    C. "Although he was small, he wasn't afraid of the other bigger animals who wanted to eat him."
    D. "He jumped in and stayed underwater as long as he could. At last the wasps went away."

2. Look at the illustration in question 1 again. Which of the statements below is the most accurate description of the illustration in relation to Passage 1?

    A. The illustration does not represent the passage. While it shows the Mouse Deer and the Tiger, it does not accurately represent the way the characters look according to the text.

    B. The illustration does represent the passage. It shows the Mouse Deer and the Tiger, with the tiger in control of the situation and frightening the Mouse Deer.

    C. The illustration does not fully represent the passage. While it does show the Tiger trying to capture the Mouse Deer, it does not show how cleverly the Mouse Deer tricks the Tiger, which is a major event in the story.

    D. The illustration does represent the passage. It shows the main idea that the Tiger is the king of the forest and all the other animals must follow his lead.

3. The following question has two parts. First answer Part A. Then, answer Part B.

Part A

Select a moral for this story.

    A. Be happy with who you are.

    B. Cleverness is more important than size.

    C. Kindness is always the most important thing.

    D. Cheaters never win.

Part B

Does the illustration in question 1 support the moral?

    A. No, because it doesn't show how much bigger the tiger is.

    B. No, because it doesn't convey the cleverness of the deer mouse.

    C. Yes, because it shows that the tiger can't win by cheating.

    D. Yes, because it reveals that even different creatures can be friends.

4. What do you think an illustration that captures the main idea of this story would show? Support your answer with evidence from the text.

Passage 2: The Little Red Hen, an English Folk Tale

1   A Little Red Hen lived in a barnyard. She spent almost all of her time walking about the barnyard in her picketty-pecketty fashion, scratching everywhere for worms. She dearly loved fat, delicious worms and felt they were absolutely necessary to the health of her children.

2   A cat usually napped lazily in the barn door, not even bothering herself to scare the rat who ran here and there as he pleased. And as for the pig who lived in the sty — he did not care what happened so long as he could eat and grow fat.

3   One day the Little Red Hen found a seed. It was a wheat seed, but the Little Red Hen was so accustomed to bugs and worms that she supposed this to be some new and perhaps very delicious kind of meat. Carrying it about, she made many inquiries as to what it might be. She found it was a wheat seed and that, if planted, it would grow up, and when ripe, it could be made into flour and then into bread.

4   When she discovered that, she knew it ought to be planted. However, she was so busy hunting food for herself and her family that, naturally, she thought she ought not to take time to plant it. So she thought of the Pig — upon whom time must hang heavily and of the Cat who had nothing to do, and of the great fat Rat with his idle hours, and she called loudly: "Who will plant the seed?" But the Pig said, "Not I," and the Cat said, "Not I," and the Rat said, "Not I." "Well, then," said the Little Red Hen, "I will." And she did.

5   Then she went on with her daily duties through the long summer days, scratching for worms and feeding her chicks, while the Pig grew fat, and the Cat grew fat, and the Rat grew fat, and the wheat grew tall and ready for harvest. So one day the Little Red Hen chanced to notice how large the wheat was and that the grain was ripe, so she ran about calling briskly: "Who will cut the wheat?" The Pig said, "Not I," the Cat said, "Not I," and the Rat said, "Not I." "Well, then," said the Little Red Hen, "I will." And she did.

6   She got the sickle from among the farmer's tools in the barn and proceeded to cut off all of the big plant of wheat. On the ground lay the nicely cut wheat, ready to be gathered and threshed, but the newest and yellowest and downiest of Mrs. Hen's chicks set up a "peep-peep-peeping" in their most vigorous fashion, proclaiming to the world at large, but most particularly to their mother, that she was neglecting them.

7   Poor Little Red Hen! She felt quite bewildered and hardly knew where to turn. Her attention was sorely divided between her duty to her children and her duty to the wheat, for which she felt responsible. So, again, in a very hopeful tone, she called out, "Who will thresh the wheat?" But the Pig, with a grunt, said, "Not I," and the Cat, with a meow, said, "Not I," and the Rat, with a squeak, said, "Not I." So the Little Red Hen, looking, it must be admitted, rather discouraged, said, "Well, I will, then." And she did.

8   Of course, she had to feed her babies first, though, and when she had gotten them all to sleep for their afternoon nap, she went out and threshed the wheat.

9   After this really strenuous day Mrs. Hen retired to her slumbers earlier than usual. She would have liked to sleep late in the morning, but her chicks, joining in the morning chorus of the hen yard, drove away all hopes of such a luxury. Even as she sleepily half opened one eye, the thought came to her that to-day that Wheat must, somehow, be made into bread. She was not in the habit of making bread, although, of course, anyone can make it if he or she follows the recipe with care, and she knew perfectly well that she could do it if necessary.

10   So after her children were fed and made sweet and fresh for the day, she hunted up the Pig, the Cat and the Rat. Still confident that they would surely help her some day she sang out, "Who will make the bread?" Alas for the Little Red Hen! Once more her hopes were dashed! For the Pig said, "Not I," the Cat said, "Not I," and the Rat said, "Not I." So the Little Red Hen said once more, "I will then," and she did.

11   At last the great moment arrived. A delicious odor was wafted upon the autumn breeze. The Red Hen did not know whether the bread would be fit to eat, but — joy of joys! — when the lovely brown loaves came out of the oven, they were done to perfection. Then, probably because she had acquired the habit, the Red Hen called: "Who will eat the bread?" All the animals in the barnyard were watching hungrily and smacking their lips in anticipation, and the Pig said, "I will," the Cat said, "I will," the Rat said, "I will."

12   But the Little Red Hen said, "No, you won't. I will." And she did.

5. View the image below. How does the image compare to the text?

   A. The image illustrates the text's account of the hen doing all the work while the other animals look on.
   B. The image shows the Little Red Hen refusing to give the other animals a job.
   C. The image does not represent the text because it isn't accurate.
   D. The image shows why the Little Red Hen doesn't have time to take care of her chicks.

6. View the image below. Identify the part of the text that describes the illustration.

   A. "All the animals in the barnyard were watching hungrily and smacking their lips in anticipation, and the Pig said, "I will," the Cat said, "I will," the Rat said, "I will.""

   B. "All the while the Cat sat lazily by, giggling and chuckling. And close at hand the vain Rat powdered his nose and admired himself in a mirror. In the distance could be heard the long-drawn snores of the dozing Pig.

   C. "Poor Little Red Hen! She felt quite bewildered and hardly knew where to turn. Her attention was sorely divided between her duty to her children and her duty to the Wheat, for which she felt responsible."

   D. "She spent almost all of her time walking about the barnyard in her picketty-pecketty fashion, scratching everywhere for worms.

7. View the following image of Disney's adaptation of the story, "The Wise Little Hen." Does the illustration represent the passage in "The Little Red Hen?"

   A. Yes, because it has the same characters.

   B. Yes, because the text and the image both show how much the hen has to do.

   C. No, because the image doesn't show the frustration the hen faced when the other animals refused to work.

   D. No, because the setting of the text and the movie are different.

8. What would you identify as the moral of this text? Which of the images (from question 5, 6, or 7) **best** represents this moral? Use evidence from the text to support your answer.

   _____

   _____

   _____

   _____

COMPARE & CONTRAST THEMES/ EVENTS IN DIFFERENT CULTURAL STORIES/ MYTHS

RL.4.9 Compare and contrast the treatment of similar themes and topics (opposition or good and evil) and patterns of events (the quest) in stories, myths, and traditional literature from different cultures.

Directions: Read the passages and answer the questions below.

Passage 1 : "The Donkey, The Fox, and the Lion"
by Aesop

The Donkey and the Fox, having entered into partnership together for their mutual protection, went out into the forest to hunt. They had not proceeded far when they met a Lion. The Fox, seeing imminent danger, approached the Lion and promised to contrive for him the capture of the Donkey if the Lion would pledge his word not to harm the Fox. Then, upon assuring the Donkey that he would not be injured, the Fox led him to a deep pit and arranged that he should fall into it. The Lion, seeing that the Donkey was secured, immediately pounced on the Fox and attacked the Donkey.

Passage 2: "The Fox and the Crow"
by Aesop

1   The fox once saw a crow fly by with a piece of cheese in her beak. "I want that cheese," thought the fox.

2   He sat down beneath the tree and called, "Good day, Miss Crow. How well you are looking, how bright your eyes, how glossy your feathers." The crow was pleased. She loved to be flattered.

3   "I am sure your voice is even more beautiful than your feathers," cried the Fox.

4   "Won't you sing a song for me, O queen of the birds?"

5   The crow was so pleased that she could hardly sit still.

6   She lifted her head high, closed her eyes and opened her beak to sing. "Cawwww!"

7   The cheese fell to the ground right in front of the fox.

8   "Thank you Miss Crow," he said to the unhappy bird. "In exchange for your cheese, I will give one piece of advice: never trust a flatterer."

1. What theme is developed in Passage 1?
    A. Betraying a friend has consequences.
    B. There is no such thing as a true friendship.
    C. Animals never protect each other.
    D. True friends never leave one another.

2. What is a theme of both Passages 1 and 2?
    A. Hard work is rewarded.
    B. Foxes are not smart.
    C. Don't let your guard down.
    D. There is strength in numbers.

3. What is the main theme of Passage 2?
    A. Foxes are too lazy to get their own food.
    B. Don't trust a stranger's flattery.
    C. Crows are not smart.
    D. Stealing food from birds is easy.

4. Read Passages 1 and 2. Match the statements to compare how Aesop approaches the topic of deception in each text.
    - Aesop has a character explicitly address the topic of deception by stating the moral.

    - Aesop uses the actions of multiple characters to explore the topic of deception.

"The Donkey, The Fox, and the Lion"	"The Fox and the Crow"

5. What text structure does Aesop use to develop his topic in both passages?
    A. In "The Donkey, The Fox, and the Lion" the author uses first person narration, while in "The Fox and the Crow" the author uses setting.
    B. In "The Donkey, The Fox, and the Lion" the author uses third person narration, while in "The Fox and the Crow" the author uses dialogue.
    C. In "The Donkey, The Fox, and the Lion" the author uses characters, while in "The Fox and the Crow" the author uses setting.
    D. In "The Donkey, The Fox, and the Lion" the author uses first person narration, while in "The Fox and the Crow" the author uses dialogue.

6. How are the patterns of events in Passages 1 and 2 similar?

_____

_____

_____

_____

_____

_____

_____

_____

Passage 3: Excerpt from "The Three Little Pigs"
by Joseph Jacobs

At the beginning of this story, the wolf is trying to eat the pig.

1   The next day the wolf came again, and said to the little pig, "Little pig, there is a fair at Shanklin this afternoon. Will you go?"

2   "Oh yes," said the pig, "I will go. What time shall you be ready?"

3   "At three," said the wolf. So the little pig set off before the time as usual, and got to the fair, and bought a butter churn, which he was going home with, when he saw the wolf coming. He did not know what to do, so he got into the churn to hide, and by so doing turned it around, and it rolled down the hill with the pig in it. This frightened the wolf so much that he ran home without going to the fair. He went to the pig's house, and told him how frightened he had been by a great round thing which came down the hill past him.

4   Then the little pig said, "Ha, I frightened you, then. I had been to the fair and bought a butter churn, and when I saw you, I got into it, and rolled down the hill."

5   Then the wolf was very angry indeed, and declared he would eat up the little pig, and that he would get down the chimney after him. When the little pig saw what he was about, he hung up the pot full of water, and made a blazing fire, and, just as the wolf was coming down, took off the cover, and in fell the wolf. The little pig put on the cover again in an instant, boiled him up, and ate him for supper, and lived happily ever afterwards.

7. The following question has two parts. First answer Part A. Then, answer Part B.

Part A
What is the theme of Passage 3?
A. Working hard is the most important quality.
B. The best way to target a bully is to ignore him.
C. Using fear can help you outsmart an enemy.
D. Deception has consequences.

Part B

Which statement from the text best supports the answer in Part A?

A. "So the little pig went off before the time as usual, and got to the fair, and bought a butter churn..."

B. "Then the wolf was very angry indeed, and declared he would eat up the little pig, and that he would get down the chimney after him."

C. "He did not know what to do, so he got into the churn to hide, and by so doing turned it around, and it rolled down the hill with the pig in it."

D. "Little pig, there is a fair at Shanklin this afternoon. Will you go?"

8. How does the theme in "The Three Little Pigs" relate to the themes in Passages 1 and 2?

_____

_____

_____

_____

_____

_____

_____

_____

_____

READING: INFORMATION

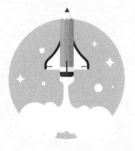

UNDERSTAND TEXT

RI.4.1 Refer to details and examples in a text when explaining what the text says explicitly and when drawing inferences from the text.

Directions: Read the passage and answer the questions below.

Passage 1: Humpback Whales

1   Humpback whales are mammals found in most of the world's oceans. Like many whales, they are endangered. The species was hunted by commercial "whalers" in the north Pacific Ocean for many years. This almost led to its extinction. In 1966 a new law made killing whales for sport or profit illegal. By that time, only about 1400 humpbacks existed. Since then, the humpback population has increased.

2   A humpback whale is easy to identify because of its stocky body and hump. Its head and mouth are covered by knobby hair follicles called tubercles. The humpback is known for its size, averaging 40-50 ft long. Females are typically larger than males. Humpbacks eat krill and small fish.

3   One feature of humpbacks is a behavior they do when they come to the surface of the ocean called breaching. When a whale breaches, it jumps out of the water. Not only does this allow the whale to breathe, scientists think it may be a social action. Breaching makes humpbacks a favorite of whale watchers.

4   Humpbacks also produce a complex song. Both females and males make sounds. But only males "sing" a long, loud song that can last up to 20 minutes. He may then repeat it for hours. Although scientists don't know exactly why the humpback sings, they believe it may be related to attracting mates, to showing authority over other male whales, or echolocation to find and identify food.

1. Based on the information in the text, which is a unique feature of humpback whales?
    A. The males are large.
    B. They are endangered.
    C. They jump out of the water.
    D. They hunt prey.

2. Why was the law in 1966 important?
    A. It likely kept humpbacks from becoming extinct.
    B. It made people start protesting that whales should not be killed for sport.
    C. It caused a decrease in the humpback whale population.
    D. It led to the discovery of why humpbacks sing.

3. Which of the following is NOT a possible reason for the humpback's song?

    A. The humpback male sings to show power over the other males.

    B. It helps the humpback find food.

    C. The song attracts females to the male whale.

    D. It scares away predators.

4. Name three characteristics that describe a humpback whale. Give evidence from the text to support your answer.

_____

_____

_____

_____

Passage 2: The Song of the Humpback

1   Male humpback whales are known for their long, loud melodies. Humpback songs can be heard over 100 miles away. They don't have vocal chords, but sing through their noses. These so-called songs are especially common in breeding season, when whales are looking for females to mate with so they can have baby whales. The entire song lasts anywhere from 10 to 20 minutes, and then the whale may repeat it over and over for hours.

2   These songs have more in common with a musical composition than you might expect. The humpback's song isn't just a random set of sounds. Instead, the song contains repeated patterns. As the whale repeats a pattern, he changes it. The song develops and changes over time.

3   Scientists have now discovered that humpbacks create a new song every year. Sometimes this is an entirely new creation. Other times, the whales will borrow parts of the previous year's song. Sometimes, they combine verses from old and new songs. The whales can switch mid-song between old and new at points where songs sound the same.

4   Whales from the same family community, or pod, sing the same song. Members of nearby pods may produce songs that are the same or similar. In fact, researchers traced one song all the way from whales in Australia to French Polynesia. They believe the song traveled from pod to pod across 4,000 miles! This is a major discovery in whale behavior. It shows that, like humans, whales exchange culture (learned behaviors) with one another.

5. The songs of male humpback whales are
    A. a random set of sounds.
    B. sung over and over.
    C. repeated by female whales.
    D. difficult to hear.

6. How are whales like humans?
    A. Their population is growing, like humans.
    B. Whale sounds can be heard as far away as human sounds.
    C. Whale songs show that music is a language understood by all.
    D. Like humans, the passing on of whale songs shows how whales share culture.

7. The following question has two parts. First answer Part A. Then, answer Part B.

Part A

Which factor is most important for when a humpback whale switches between old and new songs?

    A. parts where the songs sound similar

    B. how far the song has traveled

    C. the process is random

    D. the whale is trying to find a new mate

Part B

Which detail from the text supports the answer for Part A?

    A. "The song develops and changes over time."

    B. "The whales can switch mid-song between old and new at points where songs sound the same."

    C. "Scientists have now discovered that humpbacks create a new song every year."

    D. "These songs have more in common with a musical composition than you might think."

8. How are the songs of humpback whales shared across long distances? Use evidence from the text to support your answer.

_____

_____

_____

_____

DETERMINE MAIN IDEA & SUMMARIZE TEXT

RI.4.2 Determine the main idea of a text and explain how it is supported by key details; summarize the text.

Directions: Read the passage and answer the questions below.

Passage 1: The Greatest Swimmer of All

1   Michael Phelps is an American swimmer and champion. He has won more Olympic gold medals than anyone else in history. He competed in 5 Olympics and won gold medals in 4 Olympic Games in a row.

2   Michael's body helps him swim well. He is tall, with a long thin torso and shorter legs. His arms are very long, 6 feet 7 inches across from fingertip to fingertip. His arms act like paddles to propel him through the water. His size 14 feet are also large, and act like flippers in the water. And though his body is built for swimming, Michael worked hard for 17 years to be the best.

3   Michael retired in 2016 and didn't plan to race again. But the Discovery Channel asked him to promote Shark Week by racing a great white shark. Michael practiced for his race by racing against computer-generated reef and hammerhead sharks. On July 23, 2017, Michael Phelps faced a computer-generated great white shark. Michael swam in the pool, while the film crew inserted video of his opponent in the Atlantic Ocean.

4   A great white shark is able to swim 25 miles per hour for short amounts of time. Michael has endurance, meaning he can swim well for a long time. But although he wore a special wetsuit, Michael was no match for the shark. Michael swam 100 meters in an impressive 38.1 seconds, but the shark was faster. The shark covered the distance in 36.1 seconds. Although Michael playfully asked for a rematch, he admitted that there was "probably very little chance for me to beat him [the shark]." So who is the greatest swimmer of all time? It seems the great white shark may be the king of the seas!

1. What is the main idea of paragraph 2?
    A. Michael Phelps is is a better swimmer than a great white shark.
    B. Michael Phelps's body shape helps him be a great swimmer.
    C. Michael Phelps is the best Olympian ever.
    D. Michael Phelps has big feet that act like flippers in the water.

2. Which detail from the text best supports the title "The Greatest Swimmer of All"?
   - **A.** "It seems the great white shark may be the king of the seas!"
   - **B.** "And though his body is built for swimming, Michael worked hard for 17 years to be the best."
   - **C.** "He has won more Olympic gold medals than anyone else in history."
   - **D.** "Michael practiced for his race by racing against computer-generated reef and hammerhead sharks."

3. **Part A.**

What is the main idea in the text?
   - **A.** The great white shark swims faster than Michael Phelps
   - **B.** The Discovery Channel promoted Shark Week by racing a great white shark against Michael Phelps.
   - **C.** Michael Phelps came out of retirement to race against a shark.
   - **D.** Michael Phelps worked very hard to be the fastest swimmer in the world

Part B

Which of the following is NOT a supporting detail of that main idea?
   - **A.** "But although he wore a special wetsuit, Michael was no match for the shark."
   - **B.** "Although Michael playfully asked for a rematch, he admitted that there was 'probably very little chance for me to beat him [the shark].'"
   - **C.** "Michael swam 100 meters in an impressive 38.1 seconds, but the shark was faster."
   - **D.** "Michael swam in the pool, while the film crew inserted video of his opponent in the Atlantic Ocean."

4. Summarize the text from beginning to end in a few sentences.

_____

_____

_____

_____

_____

Passage 2: Practice Makes Permanent

1   Every 4 years, the best athletes in the world compete for gold at the Olympics. But how does an athlete become the best of the best? Training to be a great athlete may be different that you expect. Fans usually only see exciting competitions. They don't see the hours that go into training an athlete's body and mind. Athletes at the top of their sport dedicate their lives to trying to win.

2   Becoming the best in a sport involves more than just showing up at the gym every day. Athletes who want to rise to the top must commit. Training is a way of life for them. In training their bodies, athletes must build up flexibility, balance, and muscle strength. They must have the endurance to keep going.

3   Athletes must also prepare for distractions like noise and pressure. This helps them overcome distractions in competition. The best athletes can turn nervousness into positive energy. They rely on their training to get through tough competitions. Rather than think about every step, a well-trained athlete can be "in the zone." Their body knows exactly what to do from hours of practice.

4   Why can't athletes just practice their skills during competition? If an athlete wants to improve, it's important to practice over and over without the pressure of winning. In practice, he or she can concentrate on specific moves or skills. This builds muscle memory, where the athlete's body just knows what to do. During a competition, an athlete must be confident that those skills are mastered. Olympic athletes make a commitment to be the best they can be. Practice makes not only perfect, but permanent.

5. What is the main idea of this article?
    A. Top athletes must train their bodies and minds to become the best.
    B. Most athletes don't like to practice.
    C. Athletes must prepare for distractions and noise in competition.
    D. Athletes train to be fast and strong so that fans can expect an exciting competition when they perform.

6. According to the article, why do athletes prepare for distractions?
    A. to be "in the zone" during practice
    B. to help them be better than their competitors
    C. to learn to stay focused on what skills they still need to learn
    D. to make sure they are ready for unusual distractions during competition

7. The following question has two parts. First answer Part A. Then, answer Part B.

Part A

Which factor is most important for muscle memory?
- **A.** distractions like noise
- **B.** practicing a skill over and over
- **C.** being in a competition under pressure
- **D.** confidence

Part B

Which detail from the text supports the answer for Part A?
- **A.** "Becoming the best in a sport involves more than just showing up at the gym every day."
- **B.** "If an athlete wants to improve, it's important to practice over and over without the pressure of winning."
- **C.** "Olympic athletes make a commitment to be the best they can be."
- **D.** "The best athletes can turn nervousness into positive energy."

8. Based on details in the article, what does "Practice makes not only perfect, but permanent" mean? Use evidence from the text to support your answer.

_____

_____

_____

_____

USE DETAILS TO EXPLAIN EVENTS, PROCEDURES & IDEAS IN TEXT

RI.4.3 Explain events, procedures, ideas, or concepts in a historical, scientific, or technical text, including what happened and why, based on specific information in the text

Directions: Read the passage and answer the questions below.

Passage 1: Betsy Ross and the American Flag

1   Betsy Ross was born in Pennsylvania on January 1, 1752. She lived during the Revolutionary war in America. Her birthname was Elizabeth Griscom, but she went by Betsy. After completing basic schooling, she became an apprentice (someone who works for a skilled or qualified person in order to learn a trade) in a sewing shop. She learned about the sewing trade and met John Ross, who she would later marry. Betsy and John's families did not approve of the marriage because they were from different churches. Betsy was cut off from her Quaker family and joined John's church, where future president George Washington attended.

2   Betsy and John started their own upholstery, or sewing, business. Shortly after, the Revolutionary War started in America. It was hard for the sewing business to get fabric. Business was slow. With their business struggling, John joined the war. In January 1776 John Ross was killed in an explosion. He died days later.

3   Later in 1776, Betsy met with the Committee of Three. George Washington, George Ross, and Robert Morris were members of a secret committee. The men asked her to sew the first American flag. In Betsy's story, General Washington showed her a rough design of the flag. The flag would show unity against Britain in the war. According to Betsy, the flag was finished by June 1776. In July the Declaration of Independence was signed. A new nation was born: America.

4   The flag was officially adopted in 1777. It was a symbol of national unity and pride. Like the new country, Betsy's life was far from easy. She was married twice more, but her husbands died before her. Two of her children died. She lived a long life and died at the age of 84 on January 30, 1836.

1.   What happened just after the first flag was finished?
   A. The Declaration of Independence was signed.
   B. George Washington asked for Betsy Ross's help.
   C. Betsy Ross was married again.
   D. The flag was officially adopted.

2. Why did John Ross join the war?

    A. He believed in its cause.

    B. The sewing business was slow due to lack of fabric.

    C. The sewing business wasn't something he wanted to do.

    D. He thought Betsy should become a nurse.

3. What was a result of Betsy and John's marriage?

    A. Betsy had a difficult life.

    B. John joined the war to provide money for his new wife.

    C. Betsy was rejected by her church and family.

    D. Betsy learned about the sewing trade.

4. Think about two historical events: the sewing of the first flag, and the signing of the Declaration of Independence. Explain how they are connected. Give evidence from the text to support your answer.

_____

_____

_____

_____

_____

_____

Passage 2: Video Game Production

1   Have you ever thought about how your favorite video game was created? This depends on the specific game, but the basic process is the same for most games. Making a video game is a complicated, exciting task.

2   A video game begins with an idea. Ideas can come from well-known stories, characters, or may be made up. Next, a preproduction team is made. This team usually has a director, designer, engineer, artist, and writer. Each member is important. The team writes the game's story and how it will work. They decide how the game will be played and what technology will be needed.

3   Next storyboards are drawn by the artist. Each storyboard describes a scene in the game. Then, designers map out each level of play. This includes all of the different worlds a player will move through in the game.

4   After the storyboards and game designs are complete, production begins. Engineers and computer programmers write "code," a language that computers understand. Some animated games use 3D models. The game's outline is now ready. With the basics of the game set, the production team tries to make it perfect. Special effects are added.

5   After production is finished, the game goes to postproduction. Users test the first version. The engineer uses technology to fix issues. This makes the product as good as possible. Now the final product is ready to be released. Finally, the game can be bought in stores and online. Many people see this as the beginning of a game's life. Little do they know it's actually the middle of a long journey!

5. What happens right after production is finished (when postproduction begins).
   - **A.** Users rate the game as good or bad.
   - **B.** The game is sold online.
   - **C.** Users test the game.
   - **D.** The game is given special effects.

6. Which task is NOT the job of the preproduction team?
   - **A.** The team sells the game to buyers.
   - **B.** The team develops the story.
   - **C.** The team creates storyboards.
   - **D.** The team decides what technology the game needs.

7. The following question has two parts. First answer Part A. Then, answer Part B.

Part A

Why is it important to test the game before release?
   A. so that the game can be improved, if needed
   B. so that the production team can see if people like it
   C. so that customers can decide if they want to buy it
   D. so that the preproduction team can decide whether to make another game in the series

Part B

Which detail from the text supports the answer for Part A?
   A. "After production is finished, the game goes to postproduction."
   B. "The engineer uses technology to fix issues. This makes the product as good as possible."
   C. "Finally, the game can be bought in stores and online."
   D. "They decide how the game will be played and what technology will be needed."

8. Explain the production phase of creating a video game. Use information from the text in your explanation.

_____

_____

_____

_____

_____

DESCRIBE STRUCTURE OF EVENTS, IDEAS OR INFORMATION IN TEXT

RI.4.5 Describe the overall structure (e.g., chronology, comparison, cause/effect, problem/solution) of events, ideas, concepts, or information in a text or part of a text.

Directions: Read the passage and answer the questions below.

Passage 1: Is It a Cold or Allergies?

1   Achoo! As fall turns to winter, doctor's offices fill up with sneezing patients. Is it a cold? Or could it be allergies? And how can you tell the difference?

The Common Cold

2   A cold is caused by a virus that enters the body through the mouth, eyes, or nose. The virus can spread through droplets in the air when a sick person coughs or sneezes. The virus then infects the nose and throat. A cold may cause a sore throat, runny nose, cough, congestion, and sneezing.

3   Most people have two or three colds each year. There aren't many medicines that help fight a cold virus. The body relies on its immune system to get rid of the virus. The immune system works to defend the body against "attacks" by viruses or bacteria. To support the body, doctors recommend lots of fluids and rest during a cold.

Allergies

4   Allergies may seem similar to a cold, but the causes are very different. An allergy occurs when the body's immune system reacts to something the body comes in contact with. This could be something in the environment, like pollen or mold. It could also be a food, medicine, or insect sting. Allergy symptoms can include watery eyes, runny nose, sneezing, or a rash. Sometimes they even cause trouble breathing.

5   When a person encounters an allergen, their immune system makes an antibody that fights against it. This antibody is what causes symptoms. Unlike a cold, where the body eventually fights off the virus, the body will likely always react to an allergen. Allergies can be much longer lasting than a cold. But, they can be treated by avoiding allergens or with medicines that help the symptoms.

6   So how will you know if you have a cold or allergies? A short-term illness caused by contact with a virus is a cold. Allergies can't be spread from person to person and may last longer than a cold. Neither allergies or a cold are fun to experience, but understanding the differences can help you know how to respond.

1. What causes a cold?
   A. An allergen that the body contacts.
   B. A virus that infects the nose and throat.
   C. The immune system fighting something in the environment.
   D. A sore throat or runny nose.

2. What features in the text help you find information about what you are reading?
   A. Bolded words help the reader understand meanings.
   B. Diagrams label the ideas.
   C. Section headings label the ideas being compared.
   D. The title questions what the text will be about.

3. What is the overall structure of paragraph 6?
   A. compare and contrast
   B. chronological order
   C. cause and effect
   D. problem and solution

4. What concepts are being compared and contrasted? Give evidence from the text to support your answer.

_____

_____

_____

_____

_____

Passage 2: Pelé the Great

1 The name Pelé is nearly always associated with the game of soccer. Pelé was born Edson Arantes do Nascimento on October 23, 1940. He was born in Brazil, a country in South America. His father was a soccer player, and although the family was poor, Pelé showed promise in soccer from a young age. As a boy he would kick a rolled-up stocking filled with rags in place of a soccer ball.

2   Pelé showed so much talent that he tried out and earned a spot as a forward on the Santos professional soccer club in 1958 when he was only 15 years old. He scored his first professional goal before he turned 16. Soon, he was asked to play on Brazil's national team. At 17 years old, Pelé led his team to victory in the 1958 World Cup, which is the international soccer championship.

3   Pelé continued to win. He played for two more winning World Cup teams in 1962 and 1970. Pele's header against Italy in the 1970 World Cup final was his teams 100th World Cup goal. Pelé was officially the biggest goal-scorer in the history of soccer. Pelé retired from soccer in 1974. But in 1975 he came out of retirement to join the New York Cosmos, a U.S. soccer team. He led them to a championship in 1977 and retired again.

4   Although Pelé stopped playing soccer, he remains a legend. He became an ambassador for soccer. He worked to promote peace and understanding through sports. Pelé was named "Co-Player of the Century" by FIFA (International Federation of Association Football). In all, he scored 1,281 goals in 1,363 games of his career. Nearly all soccer players are measured against Pelé's legacy.

5.   What structure does the author use to present ideas?
  A. comparing Pelé to other players
  B. chronological order
  C. stating a problem and solution
  D. contrasting Pelé's career with his personal life

6.   Place the following events from the text in chronological order:

  A. Pelé was born into a Brazilian family.   1._____

  B. Pelé came out of retirement.   2._____

  C. Pelé won his first World Cup.   3._____

  D. Pelé joined his first professional soccer team. 4._____

  E. Pelé retired for the first time.   5._____

  F. Pelé became the biggest goal-scorer in history. 6._____

7. The following question has two parts. First answer Part A. Then, answer Part B.

Part A

What was a result of Pelé's second retirement?

    A. Pelé was replaced as the best player in the world.

    B. Pelé was forgotten in the world of modern soccer.

    C. Pelé changed from being only a player to having an ambassador role.

    D. Other players also met Pelé's impressive achievements.

Part B

Which detail from the text supports the answer in Part A?

    A. "In all, he scored 1,281 goals in 1,363 games of his career."

    B. "But in 1975 he came out of retirement to join the New York Cosmos, a U.S. soccer team."

    C. "He was officially the biggest goal-scorer in the history of soccer."

    D. "He worked to promote peace and understanding through sports."

8. Describe how this text is organized. Use two specific details from the text to support your answer.

_____

_____

_____

_____

_____

_____

COMPARE & CONTRAST FIRSTHAND & SECONDHAND ACCOUNTS

RI.4.6 Compare and contrast a firsthand and secondhand account of the same event or topic; describe the differences in focus and the information provided.

Directions: Read the passage and answer the questions below.

Passage 1: Excerpt from The Story of My Life
by Helen Keller

1   One day, while I was playing with my new doll, Miss Sullivan put my big rag doll into my lap also, spelled "d-o-l-l" and tried to make me understand that "d-o-l-l" applied to both. Earlier in the day we had had a tussle over the words "m-u-g" and "w-a-t-e-r." Miss Sullivan had tried to impress it upon me that "m-u-g" is mug and that "w-a-t-e-r" is water, but I persisted in confounding the two. In despair she had dropped the subject for the time, only to renew it at the first opportunity. I became impatient at her repeated attempts and, seizing the new doll, I dashed it upon the floor. I was keenly delighted when I felt the fragments of the broken doll at my feet. Neither sorrow nor regret followed my passionate outburst. I had not loved the doll. In the still, dark world in which I lived there was no strong sentiment or tenderness. I felt my teacher sweep the fragments to one side of the hearth, and I had a sense of satisfaction that the cause of my discomfort was removed. She brought me my hat, and I knew I was going out into the warm sunshine. This thought, if a wordless sensation may be called a thought, made me hop and skip with pleasure.

2   We walked down the path to the well-house, attracted by the fragrance of the honeysuckle with which it was covered. Some one was drawing water and my teacher placed my hand under the spout. As the cool stream gushed over one hand she spelled into the other the word water, first slowly, then rapidly. I stood still, my whole attention fixed upon the motions of her fingers. Suddenly I felt a misty consciousness as of something forgotten—a thrill of returning thought; and somehow the mystery of language was revealed to me. I knew then that "w-a-t-e-r" meant the wonderful cool something that was flowing over my hand. That living word awakened my soul, gave it light, hope, joy, set it free! There were barriers still, it is true, but barriers that could in time be swept away.

Passage 2: Unlocking Her World

1   When Anne Sullivan arrived at the home of Helen Keller, she found the deaf and blind young girl disconnected from the world around her. Helen had little communication and only slight understanding of her world. She was often out of control. She would kick and scream in raging tantrums. Desperate for help, Helen's parents hired Anne Sullivan from the Perkins Institute of the Blind.

2   Beginning with the word "doll," Sullivan tried to teach her young charge finger spelling. Helen liked the spelling game at first, but then grew defiant of Anne's teaching. Anne could sense that Helen didn't connect the objects to their spelling, but she pressed on.

3   With dramatic difficulty, Anne taught Helen the word "water." The teacher helped her deaf and blind young student understand the connection between the letters and the liquid by taking Helen outside to the water pump. Placing one of Helen's hands under the flowing water, Sullivan spelled out w-a-t-e-r in her other hand. And suddenly, it clicked. Helen understood what her teacher was doing. The spelling game was no longer a game, but the key to understanding her world. By that evening, Helen had learned 30 words.

1. Passage 1 is told as a
    A. firsthand account
    B. secondhand account
    C. secondary account
    D. biography

2. Who is providing the information in Passage 1?
    A. Anne Sullivan
    B. Helen Keller
    C. Helen's mother
    D. an unknown source

3. What is the author emphasizing mostly in the secondhand account (Passage 2)?
    A. the difficulty of being deaf and mute
    B. Anne's inexperience teaching the blind
    C. Helen's unwillingness to learn
    D. the importance of Anne helping Helen understand

4. What detail did the author of Passage 2 provide to show the difference between Helen's perspective and Anne's?
    A. She explains how difficult it was for Anne to help Helen connect spelling to words.
    B. She explains how Anne tried to make spelling fun for Helen.
    C. She gives examples of many different words that Anne tried to teach before Helen understood "water."
    D. She proves that Anne believed in Helen even when Helen had given up on herself.

5. Explain how the firsthand and secondhand accounts are similar and different. Use details from both accounts in your answer. Give evidence from the text to support your answer.

_____

_____

_____

_____

_____

_____

6. Compare and contrast Passage 1 and Passage 2 by writing the phrases into a Venn Diagram.

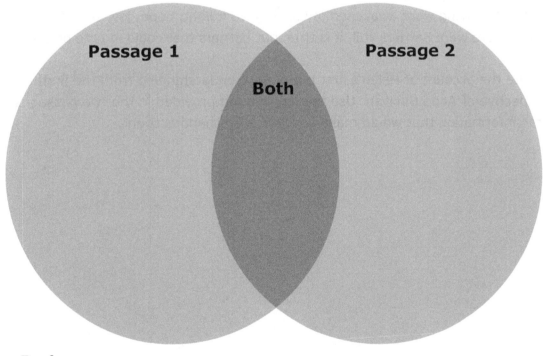

Answer Bank:

about Helen Keller

background information

describes how Helen learned words

firsthand account

gives facts

secondhand account

shows emotion

single, specific memory

7. The following question has two parts. First answer Part A. Then, answer Part B.

Part A

What is the effect of the firsthand account told from Helen's perspective?

A. It tells the reader why she disliked Anne Sullivan at first.

B. It shows her emotions regarding the experience of understanding language.

C. It explains the impact that Helen Keller made on the world.

D. It gives facts about the event.

Part B

Which **two** details from the text support the answer in Part A?

A. "Earlier in the day we had had a tussle over the words "m-u-g" and "w-a-t-e-r.'"

B. "We walked down the path to the well-house, attracted by the fragrance of the honeysuckle with which it was covered."

C. "This thought, if a wordless sensation may be called a thought, made me hop and skip with pleasure."

D. "That living word awakened my soul, gave it light, hope, joy, set it free!"

E. "There were barriers still, it is true, but barriers that could in time be swept away."

8. Rewrite the account of Helen's first moment of understanding from the firsthand perspective of Anne Sullivan. Use the information provided in the two passages and add some information that would make sense in a firsthand account.

USE IMAGES/DIAGRAMS TO UNDERSTAND TEXT

RI.4.7 Interpret information presented visually, orally, or quantitatively (e.g., in charts, graphs, diagrams, timelines, animations, or interactive elements on Web pages) and explain how the information contributes to an understanding of the text in which it appears.

Directions: Read the passage, study the graph, and answer the questions below.

Passage 1: How Much Sugar?

Toby conducted an experiment to test how much glucose, or sugar, was in various drinks. He followed the procedure below.

1. Pour a small amount of each drink into a small glass beaker. Pour enough that the entire test strip can be covered in the drink.
2. Dip one glucose test strip (obtained from a pharmacy) into each the first liquid. Completely cover the strip's test area.
3. Remove the strip from the liquid and lay it on a solid white background. This will make it easier to see what color the test strip has turned.
4. Wait exactly 30 seconds, then match the color of the test strip to a color-coded chart which measures the glucose concentration (glucose per 20 ounces of liquid).
5. Repeat with each liquid.

After he was done with the experiment, he put the results into the graph below.

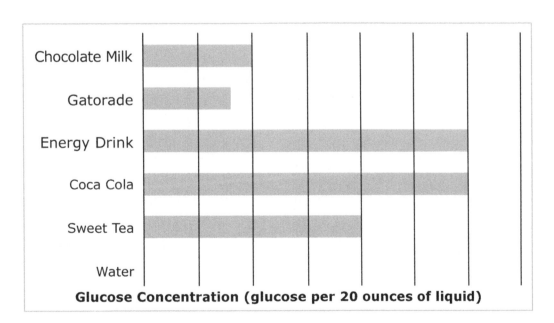

1. Place the following drinks in order from least amount of glucose to most.

   A. Gatorade

   B. Chocolate Milk

   C. Coca Cola

   D. Water

Least _____ _____ _____ _____ **Most**

2. What was the main objective of Toby's experiment?

   A. to show that Gatorade is healthier than soda

   B. to argue against children drinking energy drinks

   C. to compare the amount of glucose in drinks

   D. to create an experiment with drinks

3. Which two beverages have approximately the same about of glucose?

   A. Coca Cola and Energy Drink

   B. Sweet Tea and Chocolate Milk

   C. Water and Gatorade

   D. Energy Drink and Sweet Tea

4. How did Toby determine which beverage(s) had the most amount of glucose? Give evidence from the text to support your answer.

_____

_____

_____

_____

_____

_____

Passage 2: A Day at Band Camp

Read the schedule, then help Judy, Jack, Ryan, and Kelly plan their day at Band Camp.

> After students register, they should go to the main rehearsal room and sit with their instrument section.
>
> | | |
> |---|---|
> | **8:00 am** | Arrival and registration |
> | **8:30 am** | Group tuning and warm-up |
> | **9:15 am** | Station 1- Instrument section time with the conductor |
> | **10:00 am** | Station 2 - Team building |
> | **10:45 am** | Station 3 - Sight-reading music practice |
> | **11:30 am** | Station 4 - Rhythm games |
> | **12:15 pm** | Lunch |
> | **1:30 pm** | Station 5 - Try out a new instrument |
> | **2:15 pm** | Station 6 - Rehearse with your instrument family |
> | **3:00 pm** | Group rehearsal |
> | **4:00 pm** | Final performance for family and friends |

5. What should musicians do when they arrive in the morning?
   - **A.** begin warming up and practicing their music
   - **B.** register and sit with their instrument section
   - **C.** tune their instruments
   - **D.** find their friends

6. What time is the final rehearsal of the day?
   - **A.** 1:30 pm
   - **B.** 2:15 pm
   - **C.** 3:00 pm
   - **D.** 4:00 pm

7. The following question has two parts. First answer Part A. Then, answer Part B.

Part A

Ryan and his mom are stuck in traffic on the way to Band Camp. It is 8:10 am and they estimate it will take another 15 minutes to arrive. Will Ryan make it in time for the beginning of camp?

A. Yes, with 5 minutes left to register.

B. Yes, but without any time to register.

C. No, Ryan will arrive in the middle of warm-up.

D. No, Ryan will miss part of Station 1.

Part B

Which detail from the text supports the answer in Part A?

A. Group tuning and warm-up lasts until 9:15 am.

B. Team building occurs after Station 1.

C. Station 1 begins at 9:15 am.

D. Registration lasts until 8:30 am.

8. The conductor would like to meet with all trumpet players from 1:15-2:45 pm. Kelly plays trumpet. What parts of camp will she miss? Use information from the schedule to support your answer.

_____

_____

_____

_____

_____

_____

_____

EXPLAIN HOW AUTHORS USE EVIDENCE TO SUPPORT POINT OF VIEW

RI.4.8 Explain how an author uses reasons and evidence to support particular points in a text.

Directions: Read the passage and answer the questions below.

Passage 1: Biomimicry

1   Have you ever wondered where inventors get their ideas? Would you be surprised to know many of them come from nature? Plants and animals adapt to their surroundings in order to survive. A kind of science called biomimicry looks at how humans can learn from nature and apply it to our own lives. Bio means "life," and mimic means "to copy." So, with biomimicry we copy the best parts of nature to solve human problems.

2   Maybe the most famous example of biomimicry is Velcro. The inventor of Velcro noticed that when his dog ran through a field, he became covered in burr seeds. These burrs were so hard to pick off that he looked at one under a microscope. He noticed that the burr had tiny hooks that would catch on fibers like his dog's hair. He invented Velcro with similar hooks and loops to attach things together.

3   Another example from nature is from thorns. The long, thorny stems of a briar patch protect the plant from predators. Humans developed barbed wire to for protection too. On a farm, barbed wire keeps livestock in, and predators out.

4   Humans mimic animal adaptations too. For example, a human problem is that biking and skateboarding are dangerous. If we look at nature, the turtle has a hard shell to protect its body from predators. So, a solution to the human problem copies turtle shells, giving us helmets. Camouflage is a similar adaptation humans adopted.

5   People are constantly inventing new things that make our life safer and easier. By looking at nature, we can see how animals and plants have already adapted. Using these ideas we can work together with nature to make our lives less challenging. So the next time you encounter a problem, think about whether the issue has already been solved... in nature!

1.   What main point is the author trying to make?
     A. Animals and plants survive because they adapt to the environment.
     B. Animals are easier for humans to copy than plants.
     C. A famous inventor used biomimicry to create Velcro.
     D. Humans copy nature to make our lives better.

2. Identify one fact that the author uses to support her point that nature can give us ideas that help us stay safe.

   A. Bicycle helmets are modeled after turtle shells to protect the head from danger.

   B. Velcro is adapted from burrs, which hurt animals.

   C. Bio means "life," and mimic means "to copy."

   D. People invent new things to make our lives easier.

3. Why did the author write the passage?

   A. To explain why animals and plants are interesting for humans.

   B. To convince the reader to try inventing.

   C. To explain how many human inventions come from nature.

   D. To entertain the reader with stories about inventions.

4. What evidence could the author have added to make her argument stronger?

   _____

   _____

   _____

   _____

   _____

   _____

Passage 2: Dangerous Devices

1   Cell phones are one of the most recent developments in modern technology. They make life more convenient. But they can also be a threat to safety. And smart phones with access to the internet may be even more dangerous!

2   Many studies show that cell phones put drivers at risk. People who talk on the phone while driving are 4 times more likely to have an accident than if they are not using their phones while driving. That doesn't even take into account people who text while driving.

3   Researchers studied 699 drivers who were in an accident while using their phones. The main reason for the accidents may surprise you. The problem was not that people used one hand for the phone and one for driving. Instead, the accidents were caused when the drivers became distracted by the phone call. As a result, the drivers lost concentration.

4   Unfortunately, most drivers report using their cell phone often while driving. It's especially common with young drivers. Twenty percent of 18-29 year-old drivers report using their phone regularly or fairly often while driving. This is even true for people who know it's dangerous.

5   Education will be an important part of stopping this problem. We must help people see that drivers who are distracted, whether through calls or texting, are a danger to everyone on the road.

5. Why did the author write this passage?
    A. To teach and convince the reader that driving while distracted by a phone is dangerous.
    B. To give information about the number of accidents caused by phone use.
    C. To make the reader concerned about car accidents.
    D. To investigate what might happen if people don't stop using phones at the wheel.

6. Which is a main point of paragraph 4?
    A. People don't understand how dangerous it is to use a cell phone while driving.
    B. Most people admit to using their cell phones while driving.
    C. Young drivers are especially dangerous.
    D. Education is the only way to stop people from using cell phones behind the wheel of a car.

7. The following question has two parts. First answer Part A. Then, answer Part B.

Part A
What is the author's main claim?
    A. Nearly everyone uses a cell phone while driving.
    B. There should be worse consequences for using a cell phone while driving.
    C. Driving while using a cell phone is dangerous.
    D. Drivers under 30 cause more accidents.

Part B

Which detail from the text supports the answer in Part A?

    A. "Cell phones are one of the most recent developments in modern technology."

    B. "They make life more convenient."

    C. "We must help people see that drivers who are distracted, whether through calls or texting, are a danger to everyone on the road."

    D. "Twenty percent of 18-29 year-old drivers report using their phone regularly or fairly often while driving."

8. Reread paragraph 1. What claim does the author make that isn't well supported? How might the author better support that claim?

_____

_____

_____

_____

_____

_____

_____

INTEGRATE INFORMATION FROM TWO TEXTS

RI.4.9 Integrate information from two texts on the same topic in order to write or speak about the subject knowledgeably.

Directions: Read the passage and answer the questions below.

Passage 1: The Choice to Sit

1   One evening a tired seamstress took a seat on her bus ride home. She worked long hours at the Montgomery Fair department store and she was tired. Before she reached her bus stop, the drive ordered her to move to the back of the bus. She refused, and was arrested. But why would someone be arrested for simply sitting on a bus?

2   The year was 1955. The woman's name was Rosa Parks. And she was, in fact, breaking a law. In that time, the front 10 seats of a bus were reserved for white riders. Mrs. Parks was African American. When she sat down, Parks sat in the 11th row. The bus driver ordered her to get up because the bus was getting crowded with white passengers. Black bus riders were supposed to give white riders their seats if the white seats ran out.

3   But Rosa Parks didn't think this was fair. She challenged the idea that people should be given special privileges just because of their skin color. But what could be done? After all, this was the law. Parks put herself in danger by disobeying the laws of the city. Could one person do enough to get these laws changed?

4   Race laws were called segregation, and they didn't just apply to buses. Whites and blacks were supposed to have separate bathrooms, water fountains, and even schools. They had to sit in separate parts of a restaurant. Almost always, the buildings and sections assigned to African Americans were worse than those used by white people. During the Civil Rights movement, African Americans challenged society's treatment of them, saying it was unfair. But, with laws like segregation, would the situation ever change?

5   Eventually, segregation became against the law. One of the major reasons for change was that people like Rosa Parks were willing to stand up against it. Sometimes, standing up began with the choice to sit.

Passage 2: The Legacy of Rosa Parks

1   When Rosa Parks refused the order to move to the back of the bus, she became the Mother of Civil Rights. Even before she took a stand, Parks thought segregation was unfair. Early in her life she wrote that she would "never accept" segregation. She wanted to "search for a way of working for freedom and first class citizenship."

2   Parks worked for years as a volunteer with the NAACP, an organization dedicated to helping African Americans seek equal rights. She was the secretary. By 1955 she was discouraged. She knew something major needed to happen for change to occur. When Parks refused to give up her seat on the bus, she knew she would be arrested. But she was fed up. "I suppose when you live this experience... getting arrested doesn't seem so bad."

3   Her arrest caused a community boycott. Members of the African American community refused to ride the bus, first for a day, then a month... eventually the boycott lasted over a year. She was fired from her job shortly after her arrest. This allowed her to help organize a car-pool system where riders and drivers were matched up. She traveled the country raising awareness.

4   Her efforts helped turn the local movement into a national one. And eventually the movement started by just one woman helped to change segregation laws. But the personal cost to her and her family was difficult. She and her husband both lost their jobs. No one in town would hire them so they had to move. She became stressed and sick. Still, she carried on for the cause of equality. Throughout her life, Rosa Parks tried to stand up for her own rights and those of her African American brothers and sisters.

1. Which question from Passage 1 is best answered by Passage 2?
    A. "But why would someone be arrested for simply sitting on a bus?"
    B. "But what could be done?"
    C. "Could one person do enough to get these laws changed?"
    D. But, with laws like segregation, would the situation ever change?

2. The column on the left lists some key ideas and information about Rosa Parks. One idea is found in both Passage 1 and Passage 2. One idea is found in Passage 1 only, and one idea is found in Passage 2 only. Place the ideas in the correct columns below. Please note that one idea does not belong in either column.

Important ideas about Rosa Parks	Both Passages	Passage 1	Passage 2
Rosa Parks organized a car-pool system that helped African Americans boycott the bus for years.			
Rosa Parks was tired after a long day's work when she decided not to move to the back of the bus.			
Rosa Parks believed that it was unfair for blacks and whites to have separate seats.			
Rosa Parks soon gave up fighting against inequality.			

3. Which detail in Passage 2 helped you understand the negative effect of Rosa Parks' actions on her personal life?

   A. She created a community boycott.

   B. She lost her job and became sick.

   C. She traveled the country.

   D. She was no longer allowed to ride the bus.

4. Given the information presented in these two texts, explain how Rosa Parks impacted the cause of equality. Give evidence from the text to support your answer.

   _____

   _____

   _____

   _____

5. Read the following paragraph and highlight the least important detail in this passage.
   Parks worked for years as a volunteer with the NAACP, an organization dedicated to helping African Americans seek equal rights. She was the secretary. By 1955 she was discouraged. She knew something major needed to happen for change to occur. When Parks refused to give up her seat on the bus, she knew she would be arrested. But she was fed up. "I suppose when you live this experience... getting arrested doesn't seem so bad."

6. One important detail in Passage 2 that was left out of Passage 1 is
   A. "She was fired from her job shortly after her arrest."
   B. "Even before she took a stand, Parks thought segregation was unfair."
   C. "When Parks refused to give up her seat on the bus, she knew she would be arrested."
   D. "She knew something major needed to happen for change to occur."

7. The following question has two parts. First answer Part A. Then, answer Part B.

Part A
What topic is more fully explained by Passage 1 than Passage 2?
   A. the concept of segregation
   B. the consequences on society as a result of Park's actions
   C. Park's arrest
   D. the national movement caused by the boycott

Part B
Which detail from the text supports the answer in Part A?
   A. "But Rosa Parks didn't think this was fair."
   B. "Parks put herself in danger by disobeying the laws of the city."
   C. "Whites and blacks were supposed to have separate bathrooms, water fountains, and even schools."
   D. "But, with laws like segregation, would the situation ever change?"

8. If you were to write about Rosa Parks' impact on equality, how would you decide what details were important enough to include? Is there anything in either text that the author didn't include that you think is important to write about to help the reader understand the topic?

_____

_____

_____

_____

_____

LANGUAGE

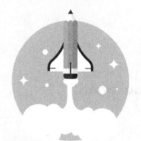

HAVE COMMAND OF GRAMMAR & USAGE

L.4.1 Demonstrate command of the conventions of standard English grammar and usage when writing or speaking.

Use Relative Pronouns and Adverbs
**L.4.1A Use relative pronouns *(who, whose, whom, which, that)*
and relative adverbs *(where, when, why)*.**

1. Identify the relative pronoun in the sentence below.
   The girl who stole your bike has been caught at her school.
   - **A.** girl
   - **B.** who
   - **C.** has been
   - **D.** her

2. Which of the following sentences correctly uses a relative pronoun?
   - **A.** He couldn't play, that surprised me.
   - **B.** She is the girl whose plays basketball.
   - **C.** A teacher is someone who helps us learn.
   - **D.** Winter is the time which it gets cold.

3. Determine the correct word for the sentence below.
   The shoes _____ Josie chose for the dance are too small.
   - **A.** that
   - **B.** who
   - **C.** where
   - **D.** what

4. Read the following sentence. Then choose the correct relative pronoun or adverb to replace the underlined error.
   We have always known that Jack is someone <u>that's talents</u> would make him famous.
   - **A.** who talents
   - **B.** whose talents
   - **C.** which talents
   - **D.** who is talents

Use Progressive Verb Tenses
L.4.1B Form and use the progressive (e.g., *I was walking; I am walking; I will be walking*) verb tenses.

1. Which of the following sentences correctly shows **present** progressive tense?
   - **A.** Our robotics team would plan a trip to Disney World.
   - **B.** Our robotics team is planning a trip to Disney World.
   - **C.** Our robotics team might plan a trip to Disney World.
   - **D.** Our robotics team will be planning a trip to Disney World.

2. Which sentence does NOT use progressive tense correctly?
   - **A.** Last year, Julian is playing soccer.
   - **B.** The color guard will be performing in the Thanksgiving parade.
   - **C.** I am going to the store with my mom.
   - **D.** We are making tacos for dinner tonight.

3. Which sentence correctly revises the sentence below by using **past progressive tense**?
   When I walked to the store, I came across a shiny penny.
   - **A.** When I walked to the store, I will come across a shiny penny.
   - **B.** When I am walking to the store, I came across a shiny penny.
   - **C.** When I walked to the store, I was coming across a shiny penny.
   - **D.** When I was walking to the store, I came across a shiny penny.

4. Complete the chart with sentences that use the appropriate progressive tenses for the phrase **I swim.**

past progressive	
present progressive	
future progressive	

Use Modal Auxiliaries
L.4.1C Use modal auxiliaries (e.g., *can, may, must*) to convey various conditions.

1. Which auxiliary verb shows a past ability to do something?
   - **A.** can
   - **B.** might
   - **C.** could
   - **D.** would

2. Which of the following sentences correctly uses a modal auxiliary verb?
   A. We would see warmer days in the summer.
   B. That branch might fall at any moment.
   C. They might study to pass the test.
   D. We were tired last night.

3. Read the following sentence. Choose the correct auxiliary verb.
   You _____ tell me how to get there so I can pick you up.
   A. couldn't
   B. may
   C. must
   D. might

4. Dan's parents tell him it is his choice whether to play in the game. Which modal auxiliary verb is correct?
   A. He would play.
   B. He can play.
   C. He must play.
   D. He will play.

Order Adjectives
L.4.1D Order adjectives within sentences according to conventional patterns
(e.g., a small red bag rather than a red small bag).

1. Which sentence correctly orders the adjectives?
   A. Julie put the brownies in a large glass plan.
   B. Allison washed her car with a round small sponge.
   C. Tiffany gave baby a plastic colorful rattle.
   D. Sarah's quilt has a square small hole in the bottom.

2. Place the adjectives below in their correct order.
   old / the / chair / wooden / rocking
   A. the old rocking wooden chair
   B. the old wooden rocking chair
   C. the wooden old rocking chair
   D. the old wooden chair rocking

3. Correct the sentence below by placing the adjectives in their correct order.
   The playset has brown, huge, long ropes for swinging.
   A. The playset has long, huge, brown ropes for swinging.
   B. The playset has brown, long, huge ropes for swinging.
   C. The playset has huge, long, brown ropes for swinging.
   D. The huge playset has brown long ropes for swinging.

Word Definitions:

Definiition of Word 1 _____

_____

Definiition of Word 2 _____

_____

Definiition of Word 3 _____

_____

Definiition of Word 4 _____

_____

3. Read the sentence below. Then identify the meaning of the suffix -ation.

   In John's determination to get the capitalization right on his spelling test, he practiced every night, earning a reputation of a good student.

   The suffix -ation means:
   A. before
   B. relating to
   C. able to
   D. action

4. Read the following excerpt from the book "Ali Baba and the Forty Thieves."

   She ran to Ali Baba in great alarm, and said: "I believe, brother-in-law, that you know Cassim is gone to the forest, and upon what account; it is now night, and he has not returned; I am afraid some misfortune has happened to him."

   How would the meaning of the excerpt change if the text said: "...I am afraid some fortune has happened to him..."?

   _____

   _____

   _____

Know How To Use Reference Materials To Clarify Word Meaning

L.4.4C Consult reference materials (e.g., dictionaries, glossaries, thesauruses), both print and digital, to find the pronunciation and determine or clarify the precise meaning of key words and phrases.

1. Reread this sentence from "Ali Baba and the Forty Thieves." Then read the dictionary entry and complete the question.

   "Their father divided a small inheritance equally between them."

   in•her•it•ance [in-**her**-i-*tuh* ns]
   noun

   1. something that is or will be inherited (given, often after death)
   2. often money or another material possession passed from parent to child or grandchild
   3. genetic characteristics passed from parent to childWhich sentence uses the meaning of the word *inheritance* as it is used in the excerpt from "Ali Baba and the Forty Thieves?" Circle **ALL** that apply.

   Inheritance is most often used as a noun.

   The children's inheritance of brown eyes were their favorite feature.

   The grandchildren's inheritance means that they can afford college.

2. Read the excerpt from "Ali Baba and the Forty Thieves."
   "Ali Baba, who expected a dark, dismal cavern, was surprised to see a well-lighted and spacious chamber..."

   Now read the dictionary entry and complete the task that follows.

   spa•cious [**spey**-sh*uh* s]
   adjective

   From the Latin word for space and the suffix -ous, meaning "full of".
   1. containing much space
   2. having a large area

   Which choice correctly identifies the pronunciation for the word *spacious*?
   - **A.** A Latin word meaning "space"
   - **B.** [spey-sh*uh* s]
   - **C.** adjective
   - **D.** spa•cious

3. Read the sentence. Then complete the chart by using a dictionary to determine how the word 'conceal' word is pronounced, which part of speech it is, and its meaning/ definition.

He climbed up a large tree, planted on a high rock, whose branches were thick enough to conceal him, and yet enabled him to see all that passed without being discovered.

Word:	conceal
Pronunciation	
Part of Speech	
Meaning/ Definition	

4. Read the three dictionary definitions for the word due. Then choose the sentence that uses it as an **adjective.**

due [doo]
adjective

1. expected to arrive at a certain time
2. required or owed

noun
3. a fee or required payment

adverb
4. referring to a compass, exactly or directly

    A. I have to pay my choir dues before the first concert.
    B. They are due to arrive at 5:00 pm.
    C. We are facing due north.
    D. Will everyone please submit their dues for basketball league?

UNDERSTAND FIGURATIVE LANGUAGE

L.4.5 Demonstrate understanding of figurative language, word relationships, and nuances in word meanings.

Understand Similes and Metaphors
L.4.5A Explain the meaning of simple similes and metaphors
(e.g., as pretty as a picture) **in context.**

1. Read the following sentence and identify the simile.
   The boy's boots were as muddy as pig's hooves as he trudged onto his mother's clean kitchen floor.
   - **A.** The boy's boots
   - **B.** as muddy as pig's hooves
   - **C.** as he trudged
   - **D.** his mother's clean kitchen floor

2. Read the following sentence, then determine the meaning of the underlined metaphor.
   The wave crashed into the shore, <u>a crumbling wall of water</u> that crushed the spectators.
   - **A.** the wave was as tall and destructive as a wall that crumbled into concrete
   - **B.** the wave was higher than the houses on the beach
   - **C.** the spectators on the shore did the wave
   - **D.** the wave was a surprise to the spectators on the beach, who thought it was actually a brick wall.

3. Read the following sentence.
   "That's how I feel too, Frosty," muttered the boy sadly as he saw the inflatable snowman laying flat as a pancake on his front lawn.
   Why does the author use the phrase "flat as a pancake" in the sentence?
   - **A.** The author helps the reader understand how the inflatable snowman became flat.
   - **B.** The author helps the reader understand what an inflated snowman looks like.
   - **C.** The author helps the reader understand why the boy is sad.
   - **D.** The author compares the boy's feelings to a deflated snowman to emphasize his sadness.

4. Rewrite the following sentence with a simile or metaphor.
   The girl's eyes are blue like her mother's eyes.

   _____

   _____

Understand Common Idioms, Adages, & Proverbs
L.4.5B Recognize and explain the meaning of common idioms, adages, and proverbs.

1. Read the sentence. Then identify the correct meaning of the idiom 'having second thoughts'.

   "Are you having second thoughts about entering the contest?"
   - **A.** going to think for a long period of time
   - **B.** having doubts
   - **C.** showing your thinking
   - **D.** explaining your reasons

2. Choose the correct word to complete the adage below.

   You can't teach an old _____ new tricks.
   - **A.** dog
   - **B.** cat
   - **C.** man
   - **D.** wizard

3. Choose the correct word to complete the adage below.

   _____ of a feather flock together.
   - **A.** Chickens
   - **B.** Eagles
   - **C.** Birds
   - **D.** Penguins

4. Read the following passage, then explain the meaning of the underlined adage.

   Julian spent all of his birthday money on candy and silly toys from the dollar store, while his twin brother Carl deposited his birthday money into his savings account. "You know, Julian," Carl lectured, <u>"a penny saved is a penny earned</u>."

   _____

   _____

   _____

   _____

Know Synonyms and Antonyms

L.4.5C Demonstrate understanding of words by relating them to their opposites (antonyms) and to words with similar but not identical meanings (synonyms).

1. Read the following passage from "The Story of Aladdin and His Magical Lamp."

   His son, who was called Aladdin, was a very careless and idle fellow. He was disobedient to his father and mother, and would go out early in the morning and stay out all day, playing in the streets and public places with idle children of his own age.

   What is an antonym of the word 'disobedient' as it is used in this passage?
   - **A.** naughty
   - **B.** respectful
   - **C.** reluctant
   - **D.** disgusted

2. This question has 2 parts. First, answer Part A. Then, answer part B.

Part A

Read the following passage.

> **Joey was disappointed by the atrocious grade on his spelling test. However, he wasn't surprised. He didn't study all week. Instead of studying, Joey played video games**.

Which detail from the passage helps the reader understand the meaning of 'atrocious' as it is used in the passage?
- **A.** "disappointed"
- **B.** "spelling test"
- **C.** "wasn't surprised"
- **D.** "played video games"

Part B

Which word has the opposite meaning of atrocious?
- **A.** bad
- **B.** excellent
- **C.** attributed
- **D.** fortunate

3. Read the following sentence.

"The child was <u>happy</u> as he unwrapped Christmas gifts."

Which of the following choices is NOT an appropriate synonym for the word happy?

    A. delighted

    B. content

    C. indifferent

    D. thrilled

4. Complete the graphic below. On the left, write words that can be used as synonyms of *small.* On the right, write words that can be used as antonyms of *small.*

Synonyms of Small
1. _____
2. _____
3. _____
4. _____

Antonyms of Small
1. _____
2. _____
3. _____
4. _____

KNOW & USE GENERAL ACADEMIC/DOMAIN-SPECIFIC WORDS

L.4.6 Acquire and use accurately grade-appropriate general academic and domain-specific words and phrases, including those that signal precise actions, emotions, or states of being (e.g., quizzed, whined, stammered) and that are basic to a particular topic (e.g., *wildlife, conservation,* and *endangered* when discussing animal preservation).

Passage 1: Ecosystems

Directions: Read the passage and answer the questions below.

1   An ecosystem is a biological community and its environment. The way that living things interact with non-living things in the environment is very important to the ecosystem. Living things include plants, animals, insects, and tiny organisms called microorganisms. The ecosystem also has non-living things like the sun, earth, soil, weather, and atmosphere.

2   An ecosystem is in balance when everything works together as it should. When the ecosystem is in balance the living and non-living things exist in harmony. But when something disturbs the balance, it's called an intruder. Intruders can include human beings, pollution, changes in migration patterns, or the introduction of outside living things. When the stability of an ecosystem is interrupted, the ecosystem can be damaged or destroyed.

1. What does the word 'harmony' mean in the context of this passage?
      A. musical
      B. stability
      C. discord
      D. living

6. The correct answer is:

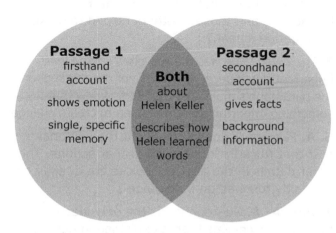

7. Part A- B. The first passage demonstrates Helen's emotions as only a firsthand account can.

Part B- C and D. These answer choices reveal Helen's emotions, about going outside and about her first experience with understanding. The other answer choices are not directly related to Helen's emotions.

8. [Suggested answer: Helen was locked in her own world. Because she understood little, she threw tantrums. I began by giving her a doll, and spelling out d-o-l-l in her hand. She liked this at first, and I taught her other spellings. But I could tell she did not connect the doll in her hand to "doll" the word. We argued over "mug" and "water." I could tell she was smart, but I needed to help her brain connect. So I took her outside, to where water was running. I placed her hand under the running water and spelled w-a-t-e-r. Her face lit up! She now knew that the wetness running down her arm was water.]

RI.4.7 Using Images/Diagrams to Understand Text

1. The correct order from least to greatest is:

Least	D	A	B	C	Most

2. A. The main objective is to compare glucose in drinks. Answer 'D" is too general. The other answer choices are incorrect.

3. C. Coca Cola and Energy Drink have the highest levels of glucose and the bar graph reaches the same point. The other answer choices are incorrect.

4. [Suggested answer: Toby dipped a test strip into each beverage, then matched the color of the test strip to the color indicated for glucose concentration. Toby graphed each beverage according to the

amount of glucose (per 20 ounces of liquid) to determine that Coca Cola and Energy Drink had the highest amount of glucose of those tested.]

5. B. The musicians should register and then sit with their instrument section. This is given in the instructions at the top of the schedule. The other answer choices are incorrect.

6. C. The final rehearsal is at 3:00 pm. Readers can infer this even though it does not say "final rehearsal" on the schedule—it is the last listed rehearsal of the day.

7. Part A- A. If Ryan will take another 15 minutes to arrive, and it is 8:10, then Ryan will arrive at 8:25 am. That will allow him 5 minutes to register and make it to the first even on time.

Part B- D. Readers must infer that registration lasts until 8:30 since there is no other event until that time. The other answer choices are irrelevant to Part A.

8. [Suggested answer: Kelly will miss the last part of Station 5 (try out a new instrument) and the beginning of Station 6 (Rehearse with your instrument family).]

RI.4.8 Explain How Authors Use Evidence to Support Point of View

1. D. The author's main point is that humans copy nature to make our lives better. Answer choice A. The other answer choices are either unsupported by the text or not the author's main point.

2. A. Bicycle helmets are an example of a human invention inspired by nature that directly relates to safety. Answer choices B, C and D do not support the author's claim that nature helps us invent things for safety.

3. C. The author's purpose is to explain how many inventions come from nature. The other answer choices are unsupported by the text.

4. [Suggested answer: The author could expand on the second adaptation mimicked from animals (camouflage), as it is mentioned but not explained. Also, the author could more clearly identify other human problems already solved through biomimicry. This would make her claim that humans imitate nature stronger.]

5. A. The purpose of the article is education and to convince the reader of the dangers of cell phone use while driving. While the author does give information about the number of accidents caused by phone use, this is a detail of the passage, not

preceding clause "last year" in tense. The other answer choices are correct.

3. D. Answer choice D shows past progressive tense through the phrase "I was walking." The other answer choices are incorrect.

4.

past progressive	I was swimming.
present progressive	I am swimming.
future progressive	I will be swimming.

L.4.1C

1. C. "Could" shows the past ability to do something. "Can" shows a present ability, while the other answer choices are conditional.

2. B. B is the only answer choice that correctly uses a modal auxiliary verb, stating that the branch could fall at any moment. The other answer choices are incorrect.

3. C. The missing word in the sentence is the word "must," showing that, in order for the speaker to pick up the subject, he or she has to provide information about how to get there. The other answer choices are incorrect.

4. B. Since Dan's parents have left him a choice, the word "can" correctly identifies the condition. The other answer choices are incorrect.

L.4.1D

1. A. The correct order of adjectives is article, number, opinion, size, age, shape, color, origin, material, and purpose. Answer choice A is the only sentence with adjectives in the correct order.

2. B. The correct order is: the (article) / old (age)/ wooden (material) rocking (purpose) chair (noun). The other answer choices are incorrect.

3. C. The correct order of the adjectives is huge (size), long (shape), brown (color). The other answer choices are incorrect.

4. B. The order is incorrect as black (color) should not come before long (shape). The other answer choices are correct.

L.4.1E

1. C. The preposition 'underneath' is correct in this sentence because it is describing a location and a single object. 'Between' is not correct as the sentence does not contain a description of multiple objects.

2. B. The prepositional phrase "of the book"

starts with the preposition "of." The object of the preposition is "book."

3. D. Prepositions are words that connect a noun or pronoun to the rest of the sentence. The noun or pronoun after the preposition is the object of the preposition. In this sentence, the object of the preposition is the noun 'Morocco'.

4. B. Here, the correct preposition is "with."

5. D. "In" is the correct preposition. The prepositional phrase begins with "in" and ends with the object of the preposition "corner."

L.4.1F

1. C. This sentence is a run-on because it includes two complete thoughts (put on your helmet AND stay safe on your bike) with no conjunction or punctuation. The other answer choices are correct.

2. B. Answer choice B correctly edits the run-on sentence by creating two sentences out of the two thoughts. The other answer choices are incorrect.

3. B. Answer choice B adds the conjunction "so" to connect the two thoughts (the sun is hot AND wear sunscreen). Answer choice A revises the sentence with punctuation, not a conjunction. Choices C and D use incorrect conjunctions.

4. Part A: The underlined sentence is a run-on sentence.

My dad needs to fix the water spout outside. **He says we need to start before it gets dark, the darkness will make it hard to see.** The sun is beginning to go down. I get my headlamp just in case we can't see.

Part B: [Answer: He says we need to start before it gets dark because the darkness will make it hard to see.]

L.4.1G Know Capitalization, Punctuation & Spelling

1. B. This sentence correctly uses the word "too" meaning "excessively."

2. C. The corrected sentence should read "There are two (the number of) dogs over there (location).

3. D. The correct sentence is "You're (you are) the best!" The other answer choices use the incorrect versions of frequently confused words.

4. [Answer: Where are you planning to spend your Christmas break?]

L. 4.2 Know Capitalization, Punctuation & Spelling

L.4.2A

1. C. The proper nouns in this sentence that should be capitalized are Joe (name), Soups & More (restaurant name), Arlington (city), and Virginia (state). No other nouns should be capitalized.

2. C. "Bakersville Elementary School" and "Mrs. Helgesen" should be capitalized because they are proper nouns. The other answer choices are correct.

3. D. "Sarah" is the only name or proper noun in the sentence so it should be capitalized.

4. [Do you and Joshua remember the name of the store where we bought Kansas City souvenirs?]

L.4.2B

1. B. Only the direct speech ("I think you have the wrong number" should be in quotation marks.

2. C. Sentence 3 is incorrect, because the entire sentence is in quotation marks. Only the direct speech should be: "I already did," I told him.

3. C. The comma belongs after the word 'wondering' and the word "said'. If the direct speech is broken up by information about who is speaking, you need a comma (or a question mark or exclamation mark) to end the first piece of speech and a full stop or another comma before the second piece (before the inverted comma or commas):

4. ["Wow! What a great experience," said Dan. "I know I'll come back."]

L.4.2C

1. **A.** A comma belongs after the coordinating conjunction in a sentence, in this case, the word "and." B has a comma after a conjunction, but the comma isn't needed because "and teasing one another" isn't an independent clause. The other answer choices are incorrect.

2. B. The comma belongs before the coordinating conjunction, "and."

3.

Independent Clause #1	Independent Clause #2	Coordinating Conjunction	Comma Placement
I'm practicing math every night	I can win the mathlete competition	so	after the word 'night'

4. [Charlie likes to listen to music on Pandora, but Cerise prefers to play games on a tablet.]

L.4.2D

1. B. The word "emphasized" should be spelled "emphasized." The other words are spelled

correctly.

2. D. The word "catch" is the only correctly spelled word. The other words should be spelled "problem," "compass," and "except."

3. D. The word "villain" is correct as written.

4.

Word	Syllables
vocal	2
proposal	3
twelve	1
inverse	2
canopy	3

L.4.3 Use Appropriate Language Conventions To Convey Ideas

L.4.3A

1. B. The word "slithered" is more precise because it shows the intensity of the motion. The sentence mentions the boy is "desperate" which matches in intensity. 'Moved' is not more precise or descriptive than crawled.

2.

Least Intense — Moist — Soggy — Drenched — Most Intense

3. D. "wise" is the most precise way to replace the word "smart" in this sentence, especially due to the fact that it is talking about elders and advice. Although the other answer choices could potentially mean "smart," none correctly match the connotation.

4. [Suggested answer: Intelligent refers to someone who has great knowledge and abilities. A person who is crafty is clever, or perhaps even sneaky.]

L.4.3B

1. C. This sentence is correctly identified as an exclamation, punctuated by an exclamation point. Some context clues in the sentence show that it is not simply a statement: "oh dear", "favorite" and "completely ruined."

2. A. This sentence is a statement, punctuated by a period. There are no context clues to make the reader think it's an exclamation, and question and command are incorrect choices.

ANSWER EXPLANATIONS

3. A. Quotation marks go around the spoken dialogue. The question mark is included inside of the quotation marks because it is part of the dialogue (the dialogue asks a question).

4. [Suggested answer: "Oh no, what am I going to do about this science project?" or "Oh no—what am I going to do about this science project?"]

L.4.3C

1. D. This is the example of informal English, primarily because of the use of the slang term "gonna."

2. C. This is the example of formal English as it uses academic vocabulary. The other answer choices are informal.

3.

Informal	Formal
What's up?	How are you?
anyways	nevertheless
blow up	explode

4. Sample letter:

12/1/2017

Mr. Johns

Tall Tree Elementary School

1234 Learning Lane

New York, New York 12345

Dear Mr. Johns,

I believe that every student in our school should have access to an iPad. It is important to understand technology in today's academic environment. iPads are a helpful tool for learning skills like coding. Furthermore, if every student had an iPad we could increase instructional time for the teacher. Thank you for considering my request.

Sincerely,
Keisha

L.4.4 Determine Meaning of Unknown Words When Reading

L.4.4A

1. Part A- C. The word "wealthy" means "rich."

Part B- The text explains that the man married a rich wife and became wealthy. This serve as a context clue for the meaning of "wealthy."

2. C. The word "distinguished" means "saw" based on the detail that Ali Baba could see the body of horsemen.

3. Ali Baba, who expected a dark, dismal cavern, was surprised to see a well-lighted and spacious chamber, which received the light from an opening at the top of the rock, and in which were all sorts of provisions, <u>bales of silk, brocade, and carpeting, piled upon one another, gold and silver ingots in great heaps, and money in bags</u>. The sight of all these <u>riches</u> made him suppose that this cave must have been occupied for ages by robbers, who had succeeded one another.

4.

My Definition	My Sentence
Provisions are things like supplies of food or clothing or equipment.	If you are going camping, you want to be sure to pack some **provisions,** including sturdy camping gear, food, drink or any other necessary supplies.

L.4.4B

1. B. Dismounted means that he climbed off of his horse. Without the prefix, it would say that he mounted, or climbed on. However, the prefix dis- means "apart," which changes the meaning.

2.

Prefix	Meaning	My Word	My Definition
mis-	ill/ incorrect	mistake	a wrong action
inter-	between	intermission	a time between to acts of a play or show
pre-	before	preschool	a school for kids before kindergarten stars
re-	again	repeat	to say again

3. D The suffix -ation means action. In the sentence, this can be see in the word "determination" (the action of being determined), capitalization (the action of capitalizing) and "reputation" (the action of being trustworthy or reputable).

4. [Suggested answer: If the prefix "mis," meaning "ill" is taken away from the word "misfortune," it would imply that something good has happened to Cassim.]

L.4.4C

1. "The grandchildren's inheritance means that they can afford college." This is the only answer choice that uses the word "inheritance" appropriately because it shows that the children will gain money from a relative to afford something (college).

2. B. [spey-shuh s] is the correct part of the dictionary entry to show the pronunciation of spacious.

3.

Word:	conceal
Pronunciation	[*kuh* n-**seel**]
Part of Speech	verb
Meaning/ Definition	to hide

4. B. This is the correct use of the word "due" as an adjective because it shows that they are expected to arrive at a certain time. Answer choices A and D use the noun form and answer choice C uses the adverb form.

L4.5 Understand Figurative Language

L.4.5A

1. B. The simile is "as muddy as pig's hooves" because it compares the boy's boots to something that shares a common feature (pig's hooves).

2. A. The metaphor compares the wave to a crumbling wall, showing its height and impact.

3. D. The simile "flat as a pancake" compares the boy's feelings to the flattened snowman.

4. [Suggested response: The girl's eyes are as blue as the sea like her mother's eyes]

L.4.5B

1. B. The idiom "having second thoughts" means that a person is having doubts.

2. A. The word "dog" correctly completes the adage "You can't teach an old dog new tricks."

3. C. The word "bird" correctly completes the adage "Birds of a feather flock together."

4. [Suggested answer: The adage a penny saved is a penny earned means that money that you save is more valuable than money that you spend right away. It means it is good to save money. It means that it is as useful to save money that you already have as it is to earn more money.]

L.4.5C

1. B. The word "disobedient" means that Aladdin didn't listen to his father and mother. Therefore, it's antonym is "respectful," which would imply

that he did listen.

2. Part A- A. The word "disappointed" reveals that the grade was not good.

Part B- B. Therefore, the opposite meaning of the word "atrocious" is "excellent."

3. C. All of the answer choices EXCEPT C (indifferent) could be used as a synonym for the word happy.

4.

Synonyms of Small	Antonyms of Small
1. miniature	1. ginormous
2. slight	2. huge
3. little	3. big
4. tiny	4. large

L.4.6 Know & Use General Academic/ Domain-Specific Words

1. B. The word "harmony" means "stability." The passage talks about how the ecosystem must be in balance, or stable, when referring to its harmony.

2. A. The phrase "everything works together" provides a context clue for the meaning of "balance," referring to how living and non-living things live together in harmony.

3. C. The word "interact" can be replaced with the word "cooperate." Thai can be inferred from the context clues in the passage that show that the ecosystem needs living and non-living things to stay in balance.

4. [Suggested answer: Stability- the balance or steadiness of how living and non-living things interact.]

5. C. This blank is best replaced with the word "assured." Julie is trying to convince her mom that she is fine.

6. A. This blank is best replaced with the word "concentrate." The context clue "Paying attention was a chore" provides the reader with this information.

7. B. This blank is best replaced with the word "embarrassment." This is supported by the context clue in the previous sentence that Julie was mortified.

ANSWER EXPLANATIONS

8. B. The word "pounded" shows how badly Julie's headache hurts. The other answer choices are incorrect.

9. D. The word "investigate" can be replaced with the word "research." Galileo wanted to perform experiments to discover how and why his theories worked.

10.

Word: principles	**Definition:** a truth or rule about how something works
Context Clue 1	"investigate those theories"
Context Clue 2	"apply them in everyday life"

PRACTICE TEST

the passage's main purpose. The author does not threaten. Answer choice 'D' is too general and not the main focus of the article.

6. B. Paragraph 4 emphasizes that even though people know cell phones are dangerous to use while driving, most people admit to using them while driving. The other answer choices are not the focus of the paragraph.

7. Part A- C. The main claim of the article is that driving while using a cell phone is dangerous. The other answer choices are incorrect or unsupported by the text.

Part B- C. This sentence shows that the reader is trying to convince her readers that using cell phones while driving is dangerous. The other answer choices are irrelevant to Part A.

8. [Suggested answer: The author states that smart phones are even more dangerous than cell phones but does not support this with evidence. The author should include evidence showing why smart phones are more dangerous (they allow access to social media, email, etc.) in order to strengthen the claim.]

RI.4.9 Integrate Information from Two Texts

1. C. The question posed in answer choice C. is answered in Passage 2 with the statement, "And eventually the movement started by just one woman helped to change segregation laws." The other choices are not directly answered in Passage 2.

2.

Important ideas about Rosa Parks	Both Passages	Passage 1	Passage 2
	Rosa Parks believed that it was unfair for blacks and whites to have separate seats.	Rosa Parks was tired after a long day's work when she decided not to move to the back of the bus.	Rosa Parks organized a car-pool system that helped African Americans boycott the bus for years.
Rosa Parks worked in politics, fighting against inequality.			

3. B. Parks lost her job and became ill as a result of her actions. The other answer choices are not direct results of her actions that affected her personally and negatively.

4. [Suggested answer: Rosa Parks affected equality for African American people by taking a stand against segregation. She refused to give up her seat and was arrested. That caused an

African American bus boycott, which she helped by organizing a car-pool for over a year. Eventually her actions and those of others helped to make segregation illegal.]

5. The detail "She was the secretary" is the least important detail because it does not directly support the paragraph's main idea that Parks knew that something important had to happen to create change.

6. A. Passage 1 doesn't highlight the personal cost that Rosa Parks suffered for her actions. The other details in the answer choices are directly or indirectly touched on in Passage 1.

7. Part A- A. Segregation is the only idea of the four answer choices that is explained in detail in Passage 1.

Part B- C. This sentence gives an example of what segregation laws included. The other answer choices are irrelevant to Part A or do not support its answer.

8. [Suggested answer: If I were writing about Rosa Parks' impact on equality, I would organize my information in a chart. I would list 1) Rosa Parks' beliefs and experiences before the bus incident, 2) Rosa Parks' actions on the bus, and 3) The results of the bus incident, both long term and short term. One thing the authors of Passages 1 and 2 did not include that I would include is information about what and when segregation laws changed.]

LANGUAGE
L.4.1 Have Command of Grammar & Usage
L.4.1A

1. B. The word "who" is the relative pronoun, identifying that the girl stole the bike. The other answer choices are incorrect.

2. C. The word "who" is the correct relative pronoun, identifying the teacher as the person who helps us learn. Answer choice A should use "which" rather than "that." Choices B and D are incorrect.

3. A. "That" is the correct word to refer to the shoes Josie chose. The other answer choices are incorrect.

4. B. "That's talents" is correctly replaced by "whose talents," with the word "whose" functioning as a relative pronoun. The other answer choices are incorrect.

L.4.1B

1. B. "Is planning" is the present progressive tense. Answer choices A and C are not progressive tense, and answer choice D is future progressive tense.

2. A. The verb "is playing" does not match the

FLORIDA STANDARDS ASSESSMENT

ELA Reading
Practice Test One

Session One

Directions: Read the passage, then answer the questions below.

Passage 1: Excerpt from Peter Pan
by J.M. Barrie

Feeling that Peter was on his way back, the Neverland had again woke into life. We ought to use the pluperfect and say wakened, but woke is better and was always used by Peter.

In his absence things are usually quiet on the island. The fairies take an hour longer in the morning, the beasts attend to their young, the redskins feed heavily for six days and nights, and when pirates and lost boys meet they merely bite their thumbs at each other.

But with the coming of Peter, who hates **lethargy**, they are all under way again; if you put your ear to the ground now, you would hear the whole island seething with life.

On this evening the chief forces of the island were disposed as follows. The lost boys were out looking for Peter, the pirates were out looking for the lost boys, the redskins were out looking for the pirates, and the beasts were out looking for the redskins. They were going round and round the island, but they did not meet because all were going at the same rate.

All wanted blood except the boys, who liked it as a rule, but tonight were out to greet their captain.

The boys on the island vary, of course, in numbers, according as they get killed and so on; and when they seem to be growing up, which is against the rules, Peter thins them out; but at this time there was six of them, counting the twins as two.

Let us pretend to lie here among the sugar-cane and watch them as they steal by in single file, each with his hand on his dagger.

They are forbidden by Peter to look in the least like him, and they wear the skins of bears slain by themselves, in which they are so round and furry that when they fall they roll. They have therefore become very sure-footed.

The first to pass is Tootles, not the least brave but the most unfortunate of all that gallant band.

He had been in fewer adventures than any of them, because the big things constantly happened just when he had stepped round the corner; all would be quiet, he would take the opportunity of going off to gather a few sticks for firewood, and then when he returned the others would be sweeping up the blood.

This ill-luck had given a gentle melancholy to his countenance, but instead of souring his nature had sweetened it, so that he was quite the humblest of the boys.

Poor kind Tootles, there is danger in the air for you tonight. Take care lest an adventure is now offered you, which, if accepted, will plunge you in deepest woe. Tootles, the fairy Tink who is bent on mischief this night is looking for a tool, and she thinks you the most easily tricked of the boys. 'Ware Tinker Bell.

Would that he could hear us, but we are not really on the island, and he passes by, biting his knuckles.

Next comes Nibs, the gay and debonair, followed by Slightly, who cuts whistles out of the trees and dances ecstatically to his own tunes. Slightly is the most conceited of the boys. He thinks he remembers the days before he was lost, with their manners and customs, and this has given his nose an offensive tilt.

Curly is fourth; he is a pickle, and so often has he had to deliver up his person when Peter said sternly, "Stand forth the one who did this thing," that now at the command he stands forth automatically whether he has done it or not.

Last come the Twins, who cannot be described because we should be sure to be describing the wrong one. Peter never quite knew what twins were, and his band were not allowed to know anything he did not know, so these two were always vague about themselves, and did their best to give satisfaction by keeping close together in an apologetic sort of way.

The boys vanish in the gloom, and after a pause, but not a long pause, for things go briskly on the island, come the pirates on their track. We hear them before they are seen, and it is always the same dreadful song:

Avast belay, yo ho, heave to,
A-pirating we go,
And if we're parted by a shot
We're sure to meet below!

Now answer the questions below. Base your answers on the passage.

1. There are two parts to this question. First answer part A, then part B.

Part A
Which of the following traits best describes Peter?
- (A) a leader
- (B) a follower
- (C) unsure
- (D) thoughtless

Part B
Which piece of evidence from the text supports the answer to Part A?
- (A) "The first to pass is Tootles, not the least brave but the most unfortunate of all that gallant band."
- (B) "We ought to use the pluperfect and say wakened, but woke is better and was always used by Peter."
- (C) "Let us pretend to lie here among the sugar-cane and watch them as they steal by in single file, each with his hand on his dagger."
- (D) "All wanted blood except the boys, who liked it as a rule, but tonight were out to greet their captain."

2. There are two parts to this question. First answer part A, then part B.

Part A

The theme of this excerpt can be summarized as:
   (A) Leaders have a great influence on their followers.
   (B) It is better to be a follower than a leader.
   (C) All children are followers.
   (D) Peter Pan is a terrible leader.

Part B

Identify a selection from this text that **best** supports the answer to Part A.
   (A) "Feeling that Peter was on his way back, the Neverland had again woke into life."
   (B) "Would that he could hear us, but we are not really on the island, and he passes by, biting his knuckles."
   (C) "The fairies take an hour longer in the morning, the beasts attend to their young, the redskins feed heavily for six days and nights, and when pirates and lost boys meet they merely bite their thumbs at each other."
   (D) "Take care lest an adventure is now offered you, which, if accepted, will plunge you in deepest woe."

3. Write the sentences on the lines below to create a summary of the passage.
   • The pirates sing their dreadful song.
   • The island starts to come to life.
   • The lost boys disappear.
   • The lost boys sense that Peter is on his way back to the island.
   • The lost boys look for Peter, the pirates look for the lost boys, the redskins look for the pirates, and the beasts look for the redskins.

   1. _____

   2. _____

   3. _____

   4. _____

   5. _____

4. What word or phrase could be used to substitute the word lethargy in paragraph 3?
   (A) energy
   (B) sadness
   (C) laziness
   (D) hard work

5. This excerpt is an example of which type of writing?
   - (A) drama
   - (B) prose
   - (C) poetry
   - (D) meter

6. Why are the lost boys forced to wear the skins of bears they once hunted?
   - (A) They have no other clothes.
   - (B) Peter Pan doesn't allow anyone to look like him.
   - (C) Tinker Bell makes them dress this way.
   - (D) They choose to dress this way.

7. Read the following selection from the passage. Then, underline **two** details that support the inference that Peter is powerful.

   Slightly is the most conceited of the boys. He thinks he remembers the days before he was lost, with their manners and customs, and this has given his nose an offensive tilt. Curly is fourth; he is a pickle, and so often has he had to deliver up his person when Peter said sternly, "Stand forth the one who did this thing," that now at the command he stands forth automatically whether he has done it or not. Last come the Twins, who cannot be described because we should be sure to be describing the wrong one. Peter never quite knew what twins were, and his band were not allowed to know anything he did not know, so these two were always vague about themselves, and did their best to give satisfaction by keeping close together in an apologetic sort of way.

8. How is the island different when Peter is not on the island than when he is on the island? Use **two** details from the passage to support your answer.

   _____

   _____

   _____

   _____

   _____

   _____

   _____

   _____

Passage 2: Excerpt from The Walrus and the Carpenter
by Lewis Carroll

The Walrus and the Carpenter
Were walking close at hand;
They wept like anything to see
Such quantities of sand:
"If this were only cleared away,"
They said, "it would be grand!"

"If seven maids with seven mops
Swept it for half a year.
Do you suppose," the Walrus said,
"That they could get it clear?"
"I doubt it," said the Carpenter,
And shed a bitter tear.

"O Oysters, come and walk with us!"
The Walrus did beseech.
"A pleasant walk, a pleasant talk,
Along the briny beach:
We cannot do with more than four,
To give a hand to each."

The eldest Oyster looked at him,
But never a word he said:
The eldest Oyster winked his eye,
And shook his heavy head —
Meaning to say he did not choose
To leave the oyster-bed.

But four young Oysters hurried up,
All eager for the treat:
Their coats were brushed, their faces washed,
Their shoes were clean and neat —
And this was odd, because, you know,
They hadn't any feet.

Four other Oysters followed them,
And yet another four;
And thick and fast they came at last,
And more, and more, and more —

All hopping through the frothy waves,
And scrambling to the shore.

The Walrus and the Carpenter
Walked on a mile or so,
And then they rested on a rock
Conveniently low:
And all the little Oysters stood
And waited in a row.

"The time has come," the Walrus said,
"To talk of many things:
Of shoes — and ships — and sealing-wax —
Of cabbages — and kings —
And why the sea is boiling hot —
And whether pigs have wings."

"But wait a bit," the Oysters cried,
"Before we have our chat;
For some of us are out of breath,
And all of us are fat!"
"No hurry!" said the Carpenter.
They thanked him much for that.

"A loaf of bread," the Walrus said,
"Is what we chiefly need:
Pepper and vinegar besides
Are very good indeed —
Now if you're ready, Oysters dear,
We can begin to feed."

"But not on us!" the Oysters cried,
Turning a little blue.
"After such kindness, that would be
A dismal thing to do!"
"The night is fine," the Walrus said.
"Do you admire the view?

"It was so kind of you to come!
And you are very nice!"
The Carpenter said nothing but
"Cut us another slice:
I wish you were not quite so deaf —
I've had to ask you twice!"

"It seems a shame," the Walrus said,
"To play them such a trick,
After we've brought them out so far,
And made them trot so quick!"
The Carpenter said nothing but
"The butter's spread too thick!"

"I weep for you," the Walrus said:
"I deeply sympathize."
With sobs and tears he sorted out
Those of the largest size,
Holding his pocket-handkerchief
Before his streaming eyes.

"O Oysters," said the Carpenter,
"You've had a pleasant run!
Shall we be trotting home again?'
But answer came there none —
And this was scarcely odd, because
They'd eaten every one.

Now answer the questions below. Base your answers on the poem.

9. There are two parts to this question. First answer part A, then part B.

Part A
How do the Walrus and the Carpenter feel about the sand?
- (A) They love how much sand there is.
- (B) They wish there was less sand.
- (C) They are annoyed that the sand hides the oysters.
- (D) The sand hurts their feet.

Part B
What evidence from the text supports the answer to Part A?
- (A) "If seven maids with seven mops/ Swept it for half a year."
- (B) "The Walrus and the Carpenter/ Were walking close at hand."
- (C) "O Oysters, come and walk with us!"
- (D) "If this were only cleared away,"/ They said, "it would be grand!"

10. There are two parts to this question. First answer part A, then part B.

Part A

How do the Walrus's and the Carpenter's actions reveal differences in their point of view?

(A) The Walrus thinks they should not eat the oysters, while the Carpenter disagrees.

(B) The Carpenter tricks the oysters, while the Walrus tries to warn them.

(C) The Walrus regrets eating the oysters, while the Carpenter doesn't.

(D) Both the Walrus and the Carpenter think twice about eating the oysters, but only the Carpenter eats them in the end.

Part B

Which two pieces of evidence from the text best supports the answer to Part A?

☐ "The eldest Oyster winked his eye/ And shook his heavy head."

☐ "No hurry!" said the Carpenter./They thanked him much for that."

☐ "I weep for you," the Walrus said.../ I deeply sympathize."

☐ "The time has come, the Walrus said,/ "To talk of many things..."

☐ "The Carpenter said nothing but/ "The butter's spread too thick!"

11. How do the old and young oysters respond to the Walrus differently?

(A) The young and old oysters are both wary of the Walrus.

(B) They old oyster tells the young oysters he is too old to join the Walrus.

(C) The old oyster refuses to join the Walrus, but the young oysters scurry to join.

(D) All of the oysters are confused by the Walrus's request to join him.

12. A theme of the poem can be stated as:

(A) People are cruel while animals are sympathetic.

(B) Young people (or creatures) shouldn't trust those they don't know.

(C) Respect your elders, because they are wise.

(D) It is wrong to take advantage of someone's trust.

13. The poem is a ballad, and uses which form for organization?

(A) prose

(B) rhyming stanzas

(C) setting

(D) characters

14. Read the following line from the 2ⁿᵈ stanza in the poem:

"I doubt it," said the Carpenter,/ And shed a bitter tear."

What word or phrase best replaces the word "**bitter**" in the context of the poem?
- (A) sour tasting
- (B) excited
- (C) rich
- (D) unhappy

15. How do the actions of the young oysters, contrasted with the old oyster, support the theme of the poem? Use text evidence to support your response.

_____

_____

_____

_____

16. Look at the following image.

Which two lines from the text does the image portray?
- ☐ "If seven maids with seven mops/ Swept it for half a year./ Do you suppose...That they could get it clear?"
- ☐ "The eldest Oyster winked his eye,/ And shook his heavy head"
- ☐ "Their coats were brushed, their faces washed,/ Their shoes were clean and neat"
- ☐ "And they rested on a rock/ Conveniently low:/ And all the little Oysters stood/ And waited in a row."
- ☐ "The time has come," the Walrus said,/ "To talk of many things..."

Directions: Read the passage, then answer the questions below.

Passage 3: The Navajo Nation

Hogans. Weaving. Southwest. Corn. What do all of these words have in common? Each of these words can be traced to the Navajo Native Americans. The Navajo lived in the southwestern deserts of the United States. Desert habitats have limited access to rain and water and no access to important resources such as buffalo and fish. However, the Navajo people learned how to **adapt** to the harsh conditions of the desert. Living in the desert impacted the types of homes the Navajo lived in, the kinds of food they had access to, the kinds of clothing they made and wore, and the kind of work they had to do in order to survive.

Desert Dwellers

The beginning of Navajo history can be traced all the way back to 1400. Believe it or not, hundreds of thousands of Navajo Native Americans are still alive today! Despite the Navajo's deadly battles with European settlers and losing much of its land to the United States Government, the Navajo Indian Reservation continues to be located in the southwestern deserts of the United States. Unfortunately, the reservation does not cover nearly the extent of land that the Navajo once inhabited. Today, the Navajo Indian Reservation is located at the borders of Arizona, New Mexico, Utah, and Colorado and spreads across approximately 25,000 square miles.

Shelter

While the majority of today's Navajo live in modern houses, this wasn't always the case. The traditional Navajo house is called a hogan. Hogans were one-room houses, usually occupying one family. Hogans were convenient for living in the desert habitat because they were composed of mud and logs. As a result of being built entirely from mud and logs, hogans kept cool in the summer, but also retained warmth during the colder, winter months. Hogans were shaped like domes and contained a door on the east side. Hogans didn't have any windows, but there was a hole in the roof that allowed for the proper exhaust of the fire pit that sat in the center of the home. The fire pit was typically utilized for cooking. There was no furniture on the hogan, so families slept on sheepskins around the fire.

Food

The unique climate of the desert makes it difficult to access particular animals, vegetables, and fruit. Furthermore, water is very limited. Therefore, the weather affected the food that the Navajo grew, hunted, and ate. The most important Navajo food was corn. The Navajo also grew squash and beans. Together, corn, squash, and beans is known as "The Three Sisters". In addition to vegetables, the Navajo did raise some livestock, such as sheep, goats, and horses, for food. Some of the Navajo living on the Navajo Indian Reservation today still farm and raise livestock today. For example, some Navajo raise goats, horses, cattle, and sheep.

Clothing

The desert climate also impacted the kind of clothing the Navajo made and wore. The Navajo are well known for their weaving. Sheep were an important resource to make weaving successful. First, the Navajo raised the sheep. Next, they sheared the wool from the sheep. After that, they spun the wool into yarn. The yarn was then dyed with plants and berries to make different colors. Last, they used a wooden loom to weave the wool. The final product could be anything from a skirt or breech cloth to a rug or blanket. Weaving is still an important part of Navajo life today.

Work

Men and women had different roles in the Navajo tribe. The men were primarily responsible for hunting, making hunting weapons, and protecting the family. On the other hand, women took on the roles of cooking, weaving, harvesting crops, and raising the children. It was important for the men and women to work together and to share the workload so that the family could survive and be well. Some Navajo women still make a living from making crafts and weaving today. Navajo people also hold more modern jobs such as teachers and police officers.

Native Americans Are Today's Americans

Many people relate Native Americans to the history or the past. They don't realize that many Native Americans still exist today! While much of the culture has adapted to fit today's standards of society, the majority of the heart of what makes each tribe unique still exists today.

Now answer the questions below. Base your answers on the passages.

17. Which of the following is not a food that the Navajo traditionally ate?
   (A) corn
   (B) squash
   (C) goats
   (D) buffalo

18. There are two parts to this question. First answer part A, then part B.

Part A

What is a main idea of the second paragraph of the passage "The Navaho Nation"?
   (A) The Navajo have always lived in the desert.
   (B) Only the Navajo Native Americans live in the desert.
   (C) It is easy for the Navajo to live in the desert.
   (D) Living in a desert environment is difficult.

Part B

Which detail from the text supports the answer for Part A?
   (A) "The beginning of Navajo history can be traced all the way back to 1400."
   (B) "Unfortunately, the reservation does not cover nearly the extent of land that the Navajo once inhabited."
   (C) "... the Navajo Indian Reservation continues to be located in the southwestern deserts of the United States."
   (D) "Believe it or not, hundreds of thousands of Navajo Native Americans are still alive today!"

19. Why was a hogan a useful shelter for desert living?
   (A) A hogan was easy to make.
   (B) Hogans protected the Navajo from the rain.
   (C) Hogans kept warm in the winter and cool in the summer.
   (D) Hogans could fit many people inside them.

20. There are two parts to this question. First answer part A, then part B.

Part A

What is the overall structure of paragraph 5 with the heading "Clothing"?
- (A) chronological
- (B) sequential
- (C) problem and solution
- (D) compare and contrast

Part B

Which detail from the passage supports the answer for Part A?
- (A) "Weaving is still an important part of Navajo life today."
- (B) "Sheep were an important resource to make weaving successful."
- (C) "The desert climate also impacted the kind of clothing the Navajo made and wore."
- (D) "After that, they spun the wool into yarn."

21. Why is the Navajo Indian Reservation much smaller than what the Navajo originally occupied?
- (A) The United States Government took land away from the Navajo Native Americans.
- (B) Most of the Navajo Native Americans moved away.
- (C) The European settlers bought the land from the Navajo.
- (D) The Navajo traded their land for food, shelter, and clothing.

22. Fill in the table below by placing an X in the box to show whether the detail represents the traditional Navajo Native Americans, the current Navajo Native Americans, or both.

	Traditional	Current	Both
The Navajo live in hogans.			
The Navajo live in the desert.			
The Navajo weave clothing and rugs.			
Some Navajo people are teachers and police officers.			
The Navajo grow vegetables and raise livestock.			
Many Navajo men and women lost their lives in battles with European settlers.			

23. What does the word 'adapt' mean in the first paragraph of the passage "The Navaho Nation"?
- (A) reject
- (B) ignore
- (C) disagree
- (D) acclimate

Passage 4: Sunny Star Up
Wish Upon the Sun

Have you ever wished upon a star? If you have, chances are that you did so during the nighttime. For it is only when the sun sets that we are able to view, with the naked eye, some of the billions of stars in our **solar system**. However, have you ever considered wishing upon the star that is in the center of our solar system? A solar system consists of a star and all the objects that travel around it. The sun is the center of the Earth's solar system. Therefore, when you wish upon a star, you can actually wish upon the sun!

How Did the Sun Form?

Before you can understand what the sun is composed of, it is important to know when and how the sun first formed. The Earth's solar system was created about five billion years ago. First, there existed a **nebula**. A nebula is a gigantic ball made of gas, dust, and ice. Next, the nebula's gravity was so strong that it pulled parts of the ball inside, toward the middle of itself. This force of gravity caused the ball to collapse and it began to spin. Then, the matter in the center of the ball increased exponentially in temperature. As a result, the sun formed. Meanwhile, the remaining dust, gas, and ice started to bunch together. These clumps would eventually form some of the solar system's comets, asteroids, planets, and moons.

Sun Size

The sun is so big that it's difficult to comprehend its size. The **diameter** of the sun is nearly 865,000 million miles. The diameter is the distance from one side of the sun to the other side of the sun. The Earth only has a diameter of approximately 8,000 miles. This means that about 1,000,000 Earths could fit inside the sun!

The sun sounds as though it's unimaginably large. However, it's actually considered a medium-sized star compared to the rest of the stars in the solar system. Some stars are even bigger than the sun. These stars are called **supergiants**. Supergiants can have diameters that are thousands of times bigger than the sun.

How Does the Sun Get So Hot?

Just like different levels of the ocean have different temperatures, different parts of the sun have different temperatures as well. For example, the part of the sun that is visible to earth measures about 10,000°F. However, at the core of the sun, temperatures can be as high as 27 million°F.

Why is the core of the sun so much hotter than the surface of the sun? The gas particles that make up the sun are packed closest together at the sun's center. This causes the particles to constantly crash into each other, forming heat and light energy. This process is called **nuclear fusion**. In this process, hydrogen changes into helium, creating the heat and light that all living beings on Earth depend on for survival.

Earth and Sun

Without the sun, life on Earth could not exist. For example, plants need the sun's light in order to make food. Animals, including humans, depend on plants for food. Additionally, the sun's heat keeps most of Earth's water in a liquid state, making water easily accessible to most living beings. The Earth also relies on the sun's energy. For instance, **solar energy** is becoming more and more popular. Solar energy is created by special equipment that transforms the sun's energy into electricity.

Significance of Our Sun Star

While the sun appears to be an ordinary star in regard to its size and place in the solar system, it is truly significant in many other ways. Most importantly, life on Earth would not exist without the sun. There would be no animals, no plants, no people, and no water. Think about it. The sun is the most important star in the Earth's solar system. Perhaps, instead of wishing upon a star next time you see one, you might thank the Earth's most important star for all it does and provides.

Passage 5: The Earth's Best Friend

Life on Earth

The Earth is the third farthest planet from the sun. The Earth is also the only planet known to have human life. The primary factor for this truth is the Earth's placement and relationship to the sun. The sun provides the perfect amount of heat, light, and energy that allow for life to exist and sustain here on Earth.

Star Structure

It may be hard to believe that Earth relies so heavily on a star. Yes, that's right. The sun is a star. The sun is basically a ball of hot gas that formed nearly five billion years ago. It has two basic regions, an inner and outer region. The outer region is composed of three main layers: the photosphere, the chromosphere, and the corona. The corona is the outermost layer of the sun. The chromosphere lies between the corona and the photosphere. The photosphere is the inner most part of the sun's atmosphere, and it is the only part of the sun that can be seen from Earth.

The inner region of the sun is also composed of three zones: the convective zone, the radiative zone, and the core. The convective zone is the outermost zone. The radiative zone surrounds the core, and the core is the centermost and hottest part of the sun.

The Sun's Gifts

The process of nuclear fusion creates the necessary gases the Earth needs in order to survive. During nuclear fusion, hydrogen is changed into helium. As a result, heat and light are **emitted** and transferred to Earth.

First and foremost, heat and light ensure the sustainment of the water cycle. Heat is needed to transform liquid water into vapor gas, causing evaporation. Evaporation then allows for the rest of the water cycle to occur. All living beings on Earth, animals, plants, humans, need water to survive.

The Earth also needs the sun's light in order for life to exist. Plants use the sun's energy to make food through a process called photosynthesis. This is important because people and animals depend on plants for food.

The sun also gives the Earth its four seasons. As the Earth orbits the sun, different parts of the Earth experience different seasons. For example, summer occurs when a portion of the planet is closest to the sun. The changing of seasons also impacts what and when various types of crops can grow.

Water, energy, food, seasons, and life. These are just four of the countless gifts the sun gives to the Earth. In this way, the sun is, without a doubt, the Earth's best friend.

Now answer the questions below. Base your answers on the passages.

24. What source would be most helpful in understanding the different layers of the sun? Explain why this source is most likely the most helpful. Use **two** details from the source to support your thinking.

_____

_____

_____

_____

_____

25. There are two parts to this question. First answer part A, then part B.

Part A

What topic is more fully explained by Passage 4 "Sunny Star Up" than by Passage 5 "The Earth's Best Friend"?
- (A) the layers of the Earth
- (B) the sun's benefits on Earth
- (C) how the sun was born
- (D) how the Earth was born

Part B

Which detail from the text **best** supports the answer in Part A?
- (A) "All living beings on Earth, animals, plants, humans, need water to survive."
- (B) "In this process, hydrogen changes into helium, creating the heat and light that all living beings on Earth depend on for survival."
- (C) "The sun is the center of the Earth's solar system."
- (D) "Next, the nebula's gravity was so strong that it pulled parts of the ball inside, toward the middle of itself."

26. What are supergiants?
- (A) another name for the sun
- (B) stars bigger than the sun
- (C) planets bigger than the Earth
- (D) planets bigger than the sun

27. In the boxes, use the numbers 1-6 to arrange the events for how the sun formed in the correct order.

#	Sentence
	The matter in the center of the ball collapsed and began to spin.
	The sun formed.
	The gravity of the nebula pulled parts of the ball inside itself.
	Dust, gas, and ice bunched together to form comets, asteroids, planets, and moons.
	A nebula existed in space.
	The center of the ball got very hot.

28. Which of the following is **NOT** a detail about the sun?
    (A) It would take 1,000,000 Earths to fit inside the sun.
    (B) The diameter of the sun is 865,000 miles wide.
    (C) The temperature of the sun's core is 27 million °F.
    (D) The sun has two layers.

29. Read the following paragraph from Passage 5 "The Earth's Best Friend". Then follow the directions.

The process of nuclear fusion creates the necessary gases the Earth needs in order to survive. During nuclear fusion, hydrogen is changed into helium. As a result, heat and light are <u>emitted</u> and transferred to Earth.

There are two parts to this question. First answer part A, then part B.

Part A
Which of these words is the closest in meaning of the underlined word, emitted?
    (A) hidden
    (B) released
    (C) kept
    (D) combined

Part B
Which of the following details from Passage 5 "The Earth's Best Friend" supports the answer in Part A?
    (A) "During nuclear fusion, hydrogen is changed into helium."
    (B) "... transferred to Earth."
    (C) "First and foremost, heat and light ensure the sustainment of the water cycle."
    (D) "The process of nuclear fusion creates the necessary gases the Earth needs in order to survive."

30. Passage 4 "**Sunny Star Up**" gives information about how the sun formed. Explain how the information in Passage 5 "**The Earth's Best Friend**" adds to the reader's understanding of the formation of the sun. Give two details from Passage 5 to support your explanation.

_____

_____

_____

_____

31. Which of the following effects does heat and light have on the water cycle?

   (A) They help evaporation to occur.
   (B) They make the ocean waters warm.
   (C) They prevent precipitation from falling.
   (D) They make condensation happen quicker.

32. Use the details below to complete the Venn diagram to show the similarities and differences between Passage 4 "**Sunny Star Up**" and Passage 5 "**The Earth's Best Friend**".

   • The Earth is the 3rd planet from the sun.
   • About 1,000,000 Earths could fit inside the sun!
   • The Earth needs the sun's light in order for life to exist.
   • The sun is basically a ball of hot gas that formed nearly five billion years ago.
   • The sun is a star.
   • The sun is composed of 2 regions: an inner region and an outer region.
   • Supergiants are stars that are bigger than the sun.
   • Solar energy is created by special equipment that transforms the sun's energy into electricity.

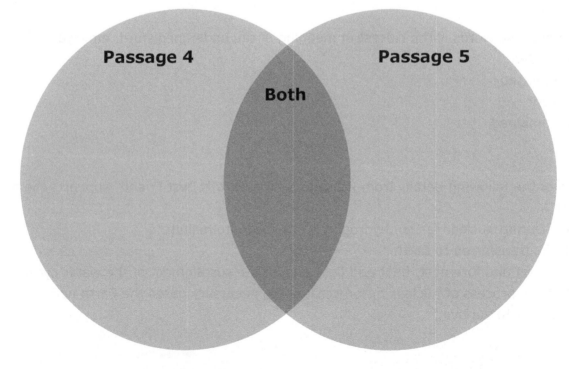

FLORIDA STANDARDS ASSESSMENT

ELA
Practice Test One
Answer Key &
Explanations

Session One

Practice Test One

Session One

Answer Explanations

1. **Part A- A; Part B- D.** Peter can be described as a leader because the island is coming to life and the boys are preparing to greet their captain. Answer choice D is the best evidence for this. The other answers choices refer either to one of the lost boys, or elements of the story that are not related to Peter's leadership.

Standard: RL.4.3

2. **Part A- A; Part B- A.** A main theme of the passage is how a leader can influence their followers. In this case, we know Peter is respected by his follows because the island is coming to life and the lost boys are preparing for his arrival. The quote in answer choice A (in Part B) is the best evidence, as it indicates the island comes to life only when Peter returns. Answer Choice C refers to how the boys and creatures go back to their normal routines when Peter is away. This is not directly as a result of Peter's influence on them. This may have been how they acted before he came to the island.

Standard: RL.4.1, RL.4.2

3. **See detailed explanation.** First: The lost boys sense that Peter is on his way back to the island.

Second: The island starts to come to life.

Third: The lost boys look for Peter, the pirates look for the lost boys, the redskins look for the pirates, and the beasts look for the redskins.

Fourth: The lost boys disappear.

Fifth: The pirates sing their dreadful song.

Standard: RL.4.1

4. **C.** Laziness is a synonym for lethargy.

Standard: RL.4.4

5. **B.** This is prose because it is a narrative text.

Standard: RL.4.6

6. **B.** Paragraph 5 states: "They are forbidden by Peter to look in the least like him, and they wear the skins of bears slain by themselves..."

Standard: RL.4.3, RL.4.1

7. **See detailed explanation.**

Possible underlined details:

-"...so often has he had to deliver up his person when Peter said sternly, "Stand forth the one who did this thing," that now at the command he stands forth automatically whether he has done it or not..."

- "...Peter never quite knew what twins were, and his band were not allowed to know anything he did not know..."

- "...so these two were always vague about themselves, and did their best to give satisfaction by keeping close together in an apologetic sort of way..."

Standard: RL.4.7

8. **See detailed explanation.** Possible answer: When Peter is not on the island, the island is quiet. Additional supporting details can be found in paragraph 1, 2 and 3. When Peter is on the island, the island is much more active and lively. We know this because Peter does not like lethargy. Additional supporting details can be found in paragraph 4.

Standard: RL.4.2

9. **Part A- B; Part B- D.** They do not like the sand because they state that it would be grand if the sand was cleared away.

Standard: RL.4.3

10. **Part A- C; Part B- 3rd and 5th Choices.** The Walrus shows remorse for eating the oysters because he states, "I weep for you." The Carpenter doesn't show remorse because he says nothing but, "The butter's spread too thick!"

Standard: XRL.4.1, RL.4.6

11. **C.** The old oyster refuses to join the Walrus, but the young oysters scurry to join.

Standard: RL.4.1

12. **B.** Young people shouldn't trust people they don't know. This is proven in the story because the oysters trust the Walrus and the Carpenter, but they are eventually eaten.

Standard: RL.4.3

13. **B.** The poem is written in rhyming stanzas.

Standard: RL.4.2

14. **D.** The word *bitter* can be replaced with the word *unhappy*. We know the Carpenter is unhappy because the beach is too sandy.

Standard: RL.5

15. **See detailed explanation.** Suggested answer: The young oysters are trusting, and easily follow the lead of the Walrus, while the older oyster seems to know he is up to no good. In return, the young oysters are tricked and eaten, while the older oyster stays safe.

Standard: RL.5

16. **4th and 5th Choices.** The image shows the Walrus and the Carpenter resting on a rock while

all of the oysters are standing in front of them, listening attentively.

Standard: RL.4.6

17. **D.** The Navajo grew corn and squash, hunted and ate goats. Buffalo did not live in the desert.

Standard: RI.4.1

18. **Part A- A, Part B- C.** The Navajo lived in the southwest region of the United States originally and continue to live on the reservation in the southwest desert today.

Standard: RI.4.2, RI.4.1

19. **C.** The mud walls kept the hogan cool in the summer and retained heat in the winter.

Standard: RI.4.1

20. **Part A- B, Part B- D.** Paragraph 5 describes the process of weaving in sequence. The word clues are "first", "next," and "last".

Standard: RI.4.5, RI.4.1

21. **A.** Paragraph 2 states: "Despite the Navajo's deadly battles with European settlers and losing much of its land to the United States Government, the Navajo Indian Reservation continues to reside in the southwestern deserts of the United States." We can infer that "lost must of its land to the United States Government" means the U.S. stole most of the Navajo's land.

Standard: RI.4.3, RI.4.1

22. **See detailed explanation.**

Traditional:

The Navajo live in hogans.

Many Navajo men and women lost their lives in battles with European settlers.

Current:

Some Navajo people are teachers and police officers

Both:

The Navajo live in the desert.

The Navajo weave clothing and rugs.

The Navajo grow vegetables and raise livestock.

Standard: RI.4.1, RI.4.3, RI.4.5

23. **D.** The Navajo *adapted* or *acclimated* to the harsh conditions of the desert.

Standard: RI.4.4

24. **See detailed explanation.** Passage 5 is the only source that provides detailed information about the structure of the sun. Student responses will vary and may include a variety of different details in their responses. For example:

-The sun has two basic regions, an inner and outer region.

-The corona is the outermost layer of the sun.

- The inner region of the sun is also composed of three zones: the convective zone, the radiative zone, and the core.

-The radiative zone surrounds the core.

Standard: RI.4.9, RI.4.1

25. **Part A- C, Part B- D.** Passage 4 has more information about how the sun was born. All of the information under the heading, *How did the sun form?*, supports this topic.

Standard: RI.4.9, RI.4.1

26. **B.** Some stars are even bigger than the sun. These stars are called **supergiants.**

Standard: RI.4.4, RI.4.1

27. **See detailed explanation.**

#	Sentence
3	The matter in the center of the ball collapsed and began to spin.
5	The sun formed.
2	The gravity of the nebula pulled parts of the ball inside itself.
6	Dust, gas, and ice bunched together to form comets, asteroids, planets, and moons.
1	A nebula existed in space.
4	The center of the ball got very hot.

Standard: RI.4.1, RI.4.3

28. **D.** The sun has 2 regions, an inner region and an outer region. Each of these regions has 3 additional layers. The sun has more than 2 layers.

Standard: RI.4.1, RI.4.9

29. **Part A- B, Part B- B.** Heat and light are *released* from the sun. We know this because they are then *transferred* to Earth.

Standard: RI.4.4, RI.4.1

30. **See detailed explanation.** Passage 5 adds information about explaining the structure of the sun. Students answer will vary and may include

various details from Passage 5. For example:

- The sun has two basic regions, an inner and outer region.

-The outer region is composed of three main layers: the photosphere, the chromosphere, and the corona.

-The inner region of the sun is also composed of three zones: the convective zone, the radiative zone, and the core.

Standard: RI.4.1, RI.4.9

31. **A.** Heat and light help the water cycle because heat is needed to transform liquid water into vapor gas, causing evaporation.

Standard: RI.4.1, RI.4.3

32. **See detailed explanation.**

Passage #4

- About 1,000,000 Earths could fit inside the sun!

- Supergiants are bigger than the sun.

-Solar energy is created by special equipment that transforms the sun's energy into electricity.

Passage #5

- The Earth is the 3rd planet from the sun.

- The sun is composed of 2 regions: an inner region and an outer region.

Both

- The Earth needs the sun's light in order for life to exist.

- The sun is basically a ball of hot gas that formed nearly five billion years ago.

- The sun is a star.

Standard: RI.4.1, RI.4.9

FLORIDA STANDARDS ASSESSMENT

Session Two

Directions: Answer the questions below:

33. Read the sentence below. Then follow the directions.

My brother asked me to help _____ with his homework.

Choose the pronoun that correctly completes the sentence.
- (A) her
- (B) it
- (C) his
- (D) him

34. Read the sentence below. Then follow the directions.

Before you play outside, you must finish your homework.

What is the prepositional phrase in the sentence above?
- (A) Before you play outside,
- (B) outside, you
- (C) you must finish
- (D) you must finish your homework

35. Choose the sentence in which the subject and verb agree.
- (A) Emmi and Valentina was selected to perform in the school's talent show.
- (B) Anna practice her math facts every day for 15 minutes.
- (C) Shay and Max both needs to go to soccer practice after school.
- (D) The damages from the hurricane show the strength of the storm.

36. Bradley wrote the following sentence.

I can't wait to go to the amusement park this weekend because I am going to eat lots of fried food and ride scary roller coasters and play lots of games and win cool prizes.

Choose the best way to fix Bradley's sentence.
- (A) I can't wait to go to the amusement park this weekend. I am going to eat lots of fried food, ride scary roller coasters, play lots of games, and win cool prizes.
- (B) I can't wait to go to the amusement park this weekend. Because I am going to eat at lots of fried food, ride scary roller coasters, play lots of games, and win cool prizes.
- (C) I can't wait to go to go to the amusement park this weekend because, I am going to eat lots of fried food, ride scary roller coasters, play lots of games, and win cool prizes.
- (D) I can't wait to go to the amusement park this weekend and I am going to eat lots of friend food, and ride scary roller coasters, and play lots of games, and win cool prizes.

Passage 6: Excerpt from Black Beauty: The Autobiography of a Horse
by Anna Sewell

Every one may not know what breaking in is, therefore I will describe it. It means to teach a horse to wear a saddle and bridle, and to carry on his back a man, woman or child; to go just the way they wish, and to go quietly.

Besides this he has to learn to wear a collar, a crupper, and a breeching, and to stand still while they are put on; then to have a cart or chaise fixed behind, so that he cannot walk or trot without dragging it after him; and he must go fast or slow, just as his driver wishes.

He must never start at what he sees, nor speak to other horses, not bite, nor kick, nor have any will of his own, but always do his master's will, even though he may be very tired or hungry; but the worst of all is, when his harness is once on, he may neither jump for joy nor lie down for weariness.

So you see this breaking in is a great thing.

I had of course been used to a halter and a headstall, and to be led about in the fields and lanes quietly, but now I was to have a bit and bridle; my master gave me some oats as usual, and after a good deal of coaxing he got the bit into my mouth, and the bridle fixed, but it was a nasty thing!

Those who have never had a bit in their mouths cannot think how bad it feels; a great piece of cold hard steel as thick as a man's finger to be pushed into one's mouth, between one's teeth, and over one's tongue, with the ends coming out at the corner of your mouth, and held fast there by straps over your head, under your throat, round your nose, and under your chin; so that no way in the world can you get rid of the nasty hard thing; it is very bad!

Yes, very bad!

At least I thought so; but I knew my mother always wore one when she went out, and all horses did when they were grown up; and so, what with the nice oats, and what with my master's pats, kind words, and gentle ways, I got to wear my bit and bridle.

Next came the saddle, but that was not half so bad; my master put it on my back very gently, while old Daniel held my head; he then made the girths fast under my body, patting and talking to me all the time; then I had a few oats, then a little leading about; and this he did every day till I began to look for the oats and the saddle.

At length, one morning, my master got on my back and rode me round the meadow on the soft grass. It certainly did feel queer; but I must say I felt rather proud to carry my master, and as he continued to ride me a little every day I soon became accustomed to it.

Passage 7: The Elves and the Shoemaker

Once upon a time there was an honest shoemaker who was very poor. He worked as hard as he could, and still he could not earn enough to keep himself and his wife.

At last there came a day when he had nothing left but one piece of leather, big enough to make one pair of shoes.

He cut out the shoes, ready to stitch, and left them on the bench; then he said his prayers and went to bed, trusting that he could finish the shoes the next day and sell them.

Bright and early the next morning, he rose and went to his workbench. There lay a pair of shoes, beautifully made, and the leather was gone! There was no sign of anyone having been there.

The shoemaker and his wife did not know what to make of it. But the first customer who came was so pleased with the beautiful shoes that he bought them, and paid so much that the shoemaker was able to buy leather enough for two pairs.

Happily, he cut them out, and then, as it was late, he left the pieces on the bench, ready to sew in the morning. But when morning came, two pairs of shoes lay on the bench, most beautifully made, and no sign of anyone who had been there. It was a puzzle.

That day a customer came and bought both pairs, and paid so much for them that the shoemaker bought leather for four pairs, with the money. Once more he cut out the shoes and left them on the bench. And in the morning all four pairs were made.

It went on like this until the shoemaker and his wife were prosperous people. But they could not be satisfied to have so much done for them and not know to whom they should be grateful.

So one night, after the shoemaker had left the pieces of leather on the bench, he and his wife hid themselves behind a curtain, and left a light in the room.

Just as the clock struck twelve, the door opened softly and two tiny elves came dancing into the room, hopped on to the bench, and began to put the pieces together.

They were quiet, but they had wee little scissors and hammers and thread. Tap! Tap! went the little hammers; stitch, stitch, went the thread, and the little elves were hard at work. No one ever worked so fast as they.

In almost no time all the shoes were stitched and finished. Then the little creatures whisked away out of the window.

The shoemaker and his wife looked at each other and said, "How can we thank the little elves who have made us happy and prosperous?"

"I should like to make them some pretty clothes," said the wife.

"I will make the shoes if you will make the coats," said her husband.

That very day they commenced their task. The wife cut out two tiny, tiny coats of green, two little pairs of trousers, of white, two bits of caps, bright red, and her husband made two little pairs of shoes with long, pointed toes.

They made the clothes as dainty as could be, with nice little stitches and pretty buttons. By Christmas time, they were finished.

On Christmas Eve, the shoemaker cleaned his bench, and on it, instead of leather, he laid the two sets of clothes. Then he and his wife hid away as before, to watch.

Promptly at midnight, the little elves came in. They hopped upon the bench; but when they saw the little clothes there, they laughed and danced for joy.

Each one caught up his little coat and things and began to put them on. They were so happy. Then, when the clock struck two, they left smiling.

They never came back any more, but from that day they gave the shoemaker and his wife good luck, so that they never needed any more help.

Now answer the questions based on the passages.

37. There are two parts to this question. First answer part A, then part B.

Part A
How does Black Beauty in Passage 6 feel toward the master?
Ⓐ appreciation for the master's gentleness
Ⓑ hatred for the master for breaking her in
Ⓒ fear of disappointing the master
Ⓓ love of being ridden by the master

Part B
Which statement supports the answer to Part A?
Ⓐ The horse feels the bit is uncomfortable in his mouth.
Ⓑ The horse remembers that his mother hated the mouth bit.
Ⓒ The master allows the horse to become used to the bit slowly.
Ⓓ The horse feels queer being ridden by the master around the pasture.

38. Place an X in the table identifying Black Beauty's response to different components of being broken in.

	Already used to	Difficult to get used to	Easy to get used to
Bit			
Halter			
Saddle			

39. Select **one** character trait that describes Black Beauty and write it in Column 1. Then select **two** sentences from the text in the list below that provides evidence for the character trait and write them in column 2.

Character Traits
Naughty
Energetic
Rude
Obedient
Guilty

Evidence

Ⓐ "…so that no way in the world can you get rid of the nasty hard thing; it is very bad!"

Ⓑ "…but I must say I felt rather proud to carry my master, and as he continued to ride me a little every day I soon became accustomed to it."

Ⓒ "…but I knew my mother always wore one when she went out, and all horses did when they were grown up; and so, what with the nice oats, and what with my master's pats, kind words, and gentle ways, I got to wear my bit and bridle."

Ⓓ "…he then made the girths fast under my body, patting and talking to me all the time…"

Ⓔ "It means to teach a horse to wear a saddle and bridle, and to carry on his back a man, woman or child…"

Column 1 Character Trait	Column 2 Evidence

40. There are two parts to this question. First answer part A, then part B.

Part A

What theme is **best** represented in Passage 7 "**The Elves and the Shoemaker**"?

Ⓐ Don't talk to strangers.

Ⓑ It is better to receive than to give.

Ⓒ Beauty is in the eye of the beholder.

Ⓓ If you do kind things for others, they will do kind things for you.

Part B

Which 2 pieces of evidence **best** support the answer to Part A?

☐ "Each one caught up his little coat and things and began to put them on."

☐ "Just as the clock struck twelve, the door opened softly and two tiny elves came dancing into the room, hopped on to the bench, and began to put the pieces together."

☐ "They never came back any more, but from that day they gave the shoemaker and his wife good luck, so that they never needed any more help."

☐ "...he and his wife hid themselves behind a curtain, and left a light in the room."

☐ "I should like to make them some pretty clothes," said the wife."

41. Read the following sentence from Passage 7 "**The Elves and the Shoemaker**":

Once upon a time there was an honest shoemaker who was very poor.

What statement **best** explains why the author chose to include this sentence?

Ⓐ It introduces the setting of the story.
Ⓑ It helps readers to get to know the main character of the story.
Ⓒ It proves to the readers that the shoemaker is lazy.
Ⓓ It builds suspense.

42. Fill in the table below to summarize the different elements in Passage 7 "**The Elves and the Shoemaker**" story.

Characters	
Setting	
Problem	
Key Events	
Solution	

43. How do you think the Shoemaker and Black Beauty feel about how another character in the story acts towards them? Explain your response using at least **one** detail from **each** passage.

_____

_____

_____

_____

_____

44. Which of the following is **NOT** a similarity of the two passages?

    (A) They both have characters that are kind.

    (B) They both have at least one character that helps another character.

    (C) They both show a story structure where a problem is presented and then solved.

    (D) They are both written from an omniscient narrator's point of view.

Directions: Read the passage, then answer the questions below.

Passage 8: That's A Tall Order

It was a cloudy, August morning in 1974. A thin tightrope weighing approximately 450 pounds lay between the North and South Towers of the World Trade Center in New York City.

A quarter mile high into the sky, a man by the name of Philippe Petit was preparing to take one of the most dangerous walks of his life.

Petit's Childhood

Philippe Petit was born on August 13, 1949 in Nemours, Seine-et-Marne, France. Petit was fascinated by circus arts such as juggling and magic from a young age.

As a child, he would perform these acts for tourists on the streets. It wasn't until the age of 16 that Petit began exploring the high wire and tightrope walking.

After a year of training, tightrope walking was incorporated into Petit's street performance acts.

How It All Started

Not exactly a rule follower, Petit was kicked out of a handful of schools by the time he was 18 years old. This trend of character would continue into adulthood as Petit began to explore more menacing and treacherous acts.

The first delinquent act that Petit pulled was in 1971 when he illegally walked on a wire between the towers of the Notre-Dame Cathedral in Paris, France. Subsequently, in 1973, he walked between the pylons of Sydney Harbor Bridge in Australia.

However, Petit was never truly satiated with these stunts and continued to pursue something more.

Planning and Preparation

Petit recalls first learning about the construction of the Twin Towers when he was reading a magazine in the waiting room of a dentist's office.

He was immediately captivated by the allure of possibly utilizing the two towers as a tight walking opportunity.

From that day forward, Petit made a point to learn as much about the Twin Towers as he could. He collected articles, conducted research, and even visited the Twin Towers in January of 1974.

Petit even closely observed the clothing of the construction workers and carried the identification of an American worker so that he and the members of his team could disguise themselves in order to gain access to the Twin Towers.

Petit and his collaborators snuck into the towers several times to study everything from the roofs and building layout to information regarding security measures.

In between his devious trips into the twin towers, Petit replicated the landscape of the Twin Towers and simulated the tight walking experience. For example, he laid a 200-ft. wire across a field in France and walked day after day with his 26 ft. long balancing pole.

For the duration of 6 years, Petit carefully planned, prepared, and practiced for what would become one of the most dangerous and risk-taking stunts he would ever perform. He could leave no stone unturned.

On the evening of August 6, 1974, Petit and his team, disguised as construction workers, trudged up 104 flights upstairs to the roof of the South Tower with hundreds of pounds of equipment in hand.

The men worked together to situate the steel cable across from the South Tower to the North Tower. This was only successful after many failed attempts with practice props such as fishing line and a bow and arrow. After several hours of manual, arduous labor, Petit was finally equipped and ready to walk.

The Walk

Shortly after 7:00 in the morning, Philippe Petit took his first steps from the South Tower onto the steel cable connected to the North Tower. With his 50-pound balancing pole in hand, 1,350 feet above the ground, Petit's stunt quickly attracted the attention of city onlookers below.

Philippe walked back and forth between the towers 8 times. He even danced, lay down, and kneeled on the wire as larger crowds of people formed and cheered Philippe on.

As Petit continued his daredevil performance, numerous police officers tried to persuade him to get off the wire. However, Petit continued his aerial tricks for 45 minutes before ceasing. Waiting for him on the other side was the police ready with handcuffs.

Consequences

Philippe Petit was ultimately arrested under various charges of trespassing and additional criminal acts related to his high wire walk. However, these charges were dropped and Petit did not have to serve any jailtime.

After the twin towers stunt, Petit was requested to perform a free tightrope walking act for the city's children in Central Park.

While the Twin Towers no longer stand, Petit's courageous walk between the towers will always stand as one of history's greatest tightrope performances of all time.

Now answer the questions below. Base your answers on the passage.

45. Read the following sentence from the passage (under the heading "Planning and Preparation").

He could leave no stone unturned.

According to the text, what does the phrase "leave no stone unturned" mean?
- (A) to carefully and completely prepare
- (B) to turn over all the stones
- (C) not to turn around
- (D) to not look back

46. There are two parts to this question. First answer part A, then part B.

Part A
Reread this sentence from the passage:
However, Petit was never truly satiated with these stunts and continued to pursue something more.

What word could be substituted for the word 'satiated' in paragraph 8?
- (A) disappointed
- (B) finished
- (C) prepared
- (D) satisfied

Part B
What phrase from the story supports the answer in Part A?
- (A) "...first delinquent act"
- (B) "...kicked out of a handful of schools"
- (C) "...walked between the pylons of Sydney Harbor Bridge"
- (D) "...continued to pursue something more"

47. What is the overall structure of paragraphs under the heading "How It All Started"?
- (A) problem and solution
- (B) cause and effect
- (C) chronological order
- (D) compare and contrast

48. What two pieces of evidence from the text support the answer to Question 47?
- ☐ Philippe Petit was born on August 13, 1949 in Nemours, Seine-et-Marne, France.
- ☐ It was a cloudy, August morning in 1974.
- ☐ Petit was never truly satiated with these stunts and continued to pursue something more.
- ☐ The first delinquent act that Petit pulled was in 1971.
- ☐ Subsequently, in 1973, he walked between the pylons of Sydney Harbor Bridge.

49. What features in the text help you find information about what you are reading?
   Ⓐ Bolded words help the reader understand meanings.
   Ⓑ Diagrams label the ideas.
   Ⓒ Section headings give information about what the section will be about.
   Ⓓ The title questions what the text will be about.

50. Look at the following image of Philippe Petit as he walks across the wire between the Twin Towers.

   Under which heading could this photograph be added and why?
   Ⓐ **How It All Started**, because it shows the beginning of Petit's walk between the Twin Towers
   Ⓑ **Consequences**, because it shows why Petit was arrested
   Ⓒ **Planning and Preparation**, because it shows the effects of his hard work in planning and preparing for the walk
   Ⓓ **The Walk**, because it shows Petit in the middle of his walk between the Twin Towers

51. What is the main idea of paragraphs under the heading "Petit's Childhood"?
   Ⓐ Petit's childhood is where his passion for tightrope walking was first realized.
   Ⓑ Petit had a difficult childhood and got in trouble quite often.
   Ⓒ Petit was born on August 13, 1949 in Nemours, Seine-et-Marne, France.
   Ⓓ As a child, he would perform circus acts for tourists on the streets.

52. What were the effects of Petit reading an article about the construction of the Twin Towers? Choose **all** answers that apply.
- ☐ Petit went to New York to help construct the Twin Towers.
- ☐ Petit collected articles, conducted research, and visited the Twin Towers.
- ☐ The Twin Towers no longer stand today.
- ☐ Petit was arrested for illegally crossing the Twin Towers on a tightrope.
- ☐ Petit was kicked out of 5 schools by the age of 18.
- ☐ Petit laid a 200-ft. wire across a field in France and walked day after day with his 26 ft. long balancing pole.
- ☐ Petit worked at the World Trade Center.

53. Reread the following selection from the passage. Then, underline **two** sentences that best show how Petit was sly.

He collected articles, conducted research, and even visited the Twin Towers in January of 1974.

Petit even closely observed the clothing of the construction workers and carried the identification of an American worker so that he and the members of his team could disguise themselves in order to gain access to the Twin Towers. Petit and his collaborators snuck into the towers several times to study everything from the roofs and building layout to information regarding security measures.

In between his devious trips into the Twin Towers, Petit replicated the landscape of the Twin Towers and simulated the tight walking experience. For example, he laid a 200-ft. wire across a field in France and walked day after day with his 26 ft. long balancing pole.

54. Summarize the text from beginning to end in a few sentences.

_____

_____

_____

_____

_____

_____

_____

Now answer the questions below:

55. Read the passage below. Then follow the directions.

Jaxson and Katie are so excited to go to the beach on _____ first
day of summer vacation. "I can't wait to build a sandcastle!" Jaxson exclaimed.
"I'm looking forward to putting my feet in the water," replied Katie.

Choose the best word to fit the blank line in the sentence above.
(A) there
(B) they're
(C) there're
(D) their

56. Read the passage below. Then follow the directions.

class, could you please take out your math books!" asked Mr. Carter. The students quickly
followed Mr. Carter's direction. "Please open to page 132 and read the problem silently to
yourself," Mr. Carter stated.

Choose the best way to fix the underlined part of the story above.
(A) "Class, could you please take out your math books!" asked Mr. Carter.
(B) "Class, could you please take out your math books." Asked Mr. Carter.
(C) "Class, could you please take out your math books?" asked Mr. Carter.
(D) class, could you please take out your math books!" asked Mr. Carter.

57. Read the passage below. Then follow the directions.

During the summer, I like to collect different objects from nature. For example, I like to collect
shells when I'm at the beach. I like to collect sea glass two. I also like to collect interesting
and unusual rocks from my background.

Choose the best way to fix the underlined part of the story above.
(A) to
(B) too
(C) 2
(D) two

FLORIDA STANDARDS ASSESSMENT

ELA
Answer Key &
Explanations
Session Two

Session Two

Answer Explanations

33. **D.** The pronoun *him* is used to replace the *noun* brother.

Standard: L.4.1.A

34. **A.** The clue word *before* indicates that the prepositional phrase is 'Before you play outside'.

Standard: L.4.1.E

35. **D.** The subject, *damages,* agrees with the verb, *show.*

Standard: L.4.1.F

36. **A.** Bradley wrote a run-on sentence. The best way to fix his sentence is to separate it into two separate sentences: I can't wait to go to the amusement park this weekend. I am going to eat lots of fried food, ride scary roller coasters, play lots of games, and win cool prizes.

Standard: L.4.1.F

37. **Part A- A, Part B- C.** Black Beauty appreciates the master's gentleness because the master allows the horse to become used to the bit slowly.

Standard: RL.4.4, RL.4.3

38. **See detailed explanation.**

	Already used to	Difficult to get used to	Easy to get used to
Bit		X	
Halter	X		
Saddle			X

Standard: RL.4.2

39. **Obedient; B and C.**

 - the clue words 'my mother always wore one and all horses did when they were grown up', indicate that Black Beauty does what she is supposed to.

- the clue words 'became accustomed to it' also indicate that Black Beauty was obedient.

Standard: RL.4.1, RL.4.3

40. **Part A- D; Part B- 3rd and 5th Choices.**

When the shoemaker and his wife realize that the elves have been helping them, they decide to return kindness to the elves by making them new clothes. As a result of their kindness, the elves wish the shoemaker and his wife good luck so that they never need help again.

Standard: RL.4.2, RL.4.1

41. **B.** The sentence helps readers to understand that despite being poor, the shoemaker is also an honest and decent person.

Standard: RL.4.1, RL.4.3

42. **See detailed explanation.**

Characters: shoemaker, wife, elves

Setting: shoemaker's house, village

Problem: the shoemaker is very poor (and/or the shoemaker is trying to find out who is making the shoes)

Key Events: 1. The shoemaker leaves the leather out on his workbench before going to bed. 2. The leather was replaced by a pair of shoes the next morning. 3. The pair of shoes sold for so much money that the shoemaker was able to buy enough leather to make 2 pairs of shoes. 4. The shoemaker left the leather out on his workbench, and the same thing happened again. This happened for several nights. 5. The shoemaker and his wife spied in the middle of the night and found elves were making the shoes. 6. The shoemaker and his wife made clothes for the elves to show their thanks.

Solution: The shoemaker finds out it is the elves that are helping him.

The elves give the shoemaker and his wife good luck so that the never needed help again.

Standard: RL.4.2, RL.4.3

43. **Answers will vary.** Suggested answer: In the Passage 'Black Beauty', the horse ifs grateful that the master is kind and gentle as he breaks her in. One example is that the master allows the horse to become used to the bit slowly. Text evidence for this includes the quote "what with my master's pats, kind words, and gentle ways, I got to wear my bit and bridle."

In the passage 'The Shoemaker and the Elves', the elves are grateful/happy when the shoemaker and his wife make clothes for them. Evidence from the passage includes sentences such as "When they saw the clothes there, they laughed and danced for joy." "They were so happy." "They never came back any more, but from that day they gave the shoemaker and his wife good luck, so that they never needed anymore help."

44. **D.** Black Beauty is written from the first person point of view.

45. **A.** To "leave no stone unturned" means to carefully and completely prepare. Some details from the passage that support this meaning are:

- he collected articles, conducted research, and visited the Twin Towers.

-Petit carefully planned, prepared, and practiced for what would become one of the most dangerous and risk-taking stunts he would ever perform.

Standard: RI.4.4

46. **Part A- D, Part B- D.** Petit wasn't satisfied with his stunts in Paris and Australia, so he continued to look for new challenges.

Standard: RI.4.4, RI.4.1

47. **C.** Paragraph 3 is structured in chronological order.

Standard: RI.4.5, RI.4.3

48. **4th and 5th choices.** The 4th and 5th answer choices use chronology to describe when important events occurred. While the 1st and 2nd answer choices use chronology, they do not appear in the paragraphs under the heading "How It All Started".

49. **C.** This passage uses headings to describe what each section will be about.

Standard: RI.4.5

50. **D.** The photograph would best be placed under the heading, **The Walk**, because it shows Petit in the act of walking between the Twin Towers.

Standard: RI.4.5

51. **A.** The paragraphs under the heading, "Petit's Childhood", informs the reader that it was as a child that Petit first realized his passion for tightrope walking.

Standard: RI.4.2

52. **2nd, 4th, and 6th choices.** As a result of reading the article about the construction of the Twin Towers, Petit began tirelessly planning his walk, practiced his walk in France, and was ultimately arrested.

Standard: RI.4.3, RI.4.5

53. **See detailed explanation.** Students should underline the following sentences to show that Petit was sly (clever, deceitful):Petit even closely observed the clothing of the construction workers and carried the identification of an American worker so that he and the members of his team could disguise themselves in order to gain access to the Twin Towers. Petit and his collaborators snuck into the towers several times to study everything from the roofs and building layout to information regarding security measures.

(Students may also underline the sentences that states: "In between his devious trips into the Twin Towers…"; however, this statement does not as specifically show how Petit was sly as the two prior sentences show.)

Standard: RI.4.1, RI.4.3

54. **See detailed explanation.** Key details that students should include in a summary are:

When Philippe Petit read an article about the construction of the Twin Towers, he immediately began planning and preparing to walk on a wire between them. He practiced and planned for six years. He successfully walked on a wire between the Twin Towers, but was ultimately arrested.

Standard: RI.4.2

55. **D.** *Their* would be the correct word to use the sentence because it is referring to Jaxson and Katie's first day of summer.

Standard: L.4.1.G

56. **C.** The sentence:

"Class, could you please take out your math books?" asked Mr. Carter. uses quotation marks, punctuation, and capitalization correctly.

Standard: L.4.2.A, L.4.2.B

57. **B.** *Too* is needed to replace *two* because it is referring to *as well* as or *also*.

Standard: L.4.1.G

BONUS
FULL-LENGTH
PRACTICE TEST

**GO TO THE FOLLOWING URL ADDRESS
TO ACCESS YOUR BONUS PRACTICE TEST.**

https://originstutoring.lpages.co/fsa-ela-grade-4/

Thank you for selecting this book.
We would be thrilled if you left us a review on
the website where you bought this book!